The
Three Conversions
in the
Spiritual Life

The
Three Conversions
in the
Spiritual Life

(Formerly: *The Three Ways of the Spiritual Life*)

From the French of

Fr. Reginald Garrigou-Lagrange, O.P.

TAN BOOKS AND PUBLISHERS, INC.
Rockford, Illinois 61105

NIHIL OBSTAT: Eduardus Can. Mahoney, S.T.D.
Censor deputatus

IMPRIMATUR: Leonellus Can. Evans
Vic. Gen.
Westmonasterii,
 die 4a Maii 1938

Reprinted by TAN Books and Publishers, Inc. in 1977 by arrangement with Burns & Oates, London. Reprinted again by TAN Books and Publishers, Inc. in 2002 under a new title: *The Three Conversions in the Spiritual Life*. (This book is presumably a translation of *Les trois conversions et les trois voies* [Paris, 1933]).

ISBN 0-89555-739-8

Cover illustration: Detail of "Pentecost" stained-glass window. Photo © Alan Brown 1993, Bardstown, KY. Cover design: Pete Massari, Rockford, IL.

Printed and bound in the United States of America.

TAN BOOKS AND PUBLISHERS, INC.
P.O. Box 424
Rockford, Illinois 61105
2002

"We have seen that the transformation of the Apostles on the day of Pentecost was like a third conversion for them. There must be something similar in the life of every Christian, if he is to pass from the way of proficients to that of the perfect. Here, says St. John of the Cross, there must be a radical purgation of the spirit, just as there had to be a purgation of the senses in order to pass from the way of beginners to that of proficients, commonly called the illuminative way. And just as the first conversion, by which we turn away from the world to begin to walk in the way of God, presupposes acts of faith, hope, charity and contrition, so it is also with the other two conversions. But here the acts of the theological virtues are much more profound: God, who makes us perform these acts, drives the furrow in our souls in the same direction, but much more deeply." (*Page* 58).

CONTENTS

TRANSLATOR'S NOTE

THE Translator makes grateful acknowledgement of Mr. Allison Peers' permission to use his translation of the works of St. John of the Cross,[1] and likewise of the leave given by Messrs. Burns Oates and Washbourne, Ltd., to use the late Mr. Algar Thorold's translation of *The Dialogue* of St. Catherine of Siena.[2]

[1] *The Works of St. John of the Cross*, translated from the critical edition of P. Silverio de Santa Teresa, C.D., and edited by E. Allison Peers. (London, Burns Oates and Washbourne, Ltd., 1934–1935.)

[2] *The Dialogue of the Seraphic Virgin Catherine of Siena*, translated from the original Italian, by Algar Thorold. (Burns Oates and Washbourne, Ltd., 1925.)

FOREWORD

THIS little book, presented in a form accessible to all spiritual souls, is in reality a synopsis of two larger works, which, however, it is not necessary to have read in order easily to understand what we have written here.

In *Perfection chrétienne et contemplation* we showed that, according to the principles formulated by St. Thomas and by St. John of the Cross, Christian perfection consists especially in charity, in the perfect fulfilment of the two great commandments : ' Thou shalt love the Lord thy God with thy whole heart and with thy whole soul and with all thy strength and with all thy mind ; and thy neighbour as thyself.'[1] In the same work it was seen that the *infused contemplation* of the mysteries of faith—the Trinity present within us, the redemptive Incarnation, the Cross, the Eucharist—is in the normal way of sanctity

Following the same principles we have treated elsewhere[2] of the purgations necessary in order to attain to the perfect love of God and one's neighbour ; showing in particular that the passive purgation of the senses marks entrance into the illuminative way, and that the purgation of the spirit marks entrance into the unitive way of the perfect.

Requests have reached us from several quarters for a brief outline of these two works, to set in clear relief the main principles of ascetical and mystical theology. We have not wished, however, simply to repeat what we had written elsewhere. Accordingly

---

[1] Luke x, 27.   [2] *L'Amour de Dieu et la Croix de Jésus.*

we intend to consider the whole subject from a point of view which is at once more simple and more sublime, and to speak here of the three periods of the spiritual life, and in particular of the three conversions which constitute the beginning of each.

A first chapter deals with the life of grace and the importance of the first conversion. Succeeding chapters treat of progress in the spiritual life, with special emphasis upon the other two conversions or transformations which mark the beginnings of the illuminative and the unitive ways respectively.

The division of spiritual progress according to the three ways, commonly accepted since St. Augustine and Dionysius, has become hackneyed, being reproduced invariably in all treatises on spirituality. But its profound truth, its meaning, its bearing, its vital interest, become apparent when it is explained by analogy with the periods of our physical life, and also —a point which is often forgotten—by comparison with the stages in the spiritual development of the Apostles. The Apostles owed their formation immediately to our Lord Himself, and their interior life ought, according to the teaching of the saints, to be proportionately reproduced in us. They are our models ; especially they are models for the priest. And every Christian ought in a sense to be an apostle, and so to live the life of Christ as to be able to communicate it to others.

The greatest emphasis in this book will be laid upon elementary truths. But we are apt to forget that the most sublime and most vital truths are precisely elementary truths, deeply studied, prayerfully considered and made the object of supernatural contemplation.[1]

[1] The *Dialogue* of St. Catherine of Siena, which we shall quote often in these pages, is a case in point. Read at the age of twenty or twenty-five, it may fail to bring home the doctrine which it

Many persons familiar with the Gospel, if asked
the question : ' Does the Gospel anywhere mention
the second conversion ? ' would probably answer in
the negative. And yet our Lord makes a very clear
statement on the subject. St. Mark relates[1] that
when Jesus had arrived at Capharnaum on His last
journey to Galilee He asked them : ' What did you
treat of in the way ? ' ' But they held their peace,'
the Evangelist tells us, ' for in the way they had
disputed among themselves which of them should
be greatest.' And in the Gospel of St. Matthew,[2]
where the same event is described, we read : ' Jesus,
calling unto him a little child, set him in the midst of
them, and said : Amen I say to you, unless you be
converted and become as little children you shall not
enter into the kingdom of heaven.' Is this not an
obvious reference to the second conversion ? Jesus
is speaking to the Apostles who have followed Him,
who have shared His ministry, who are to receive
Communion at the Last Supper, three of whom have
followed Him up to Thabor. They are in the state
of grace, and yet He speaks to them of the need of a
second conversion, if they are to enter far into the
kingdom of heaven or into the divine intimacy. And
to Peter in particular it was said :[3] ' Simon, Simon,
behold Satan hath desired to have you, that he may
sift you as wheat. But I have prayed for thee, that

expounds, seeming, as it does, to emphasize only elementary truths
and making little appeal to the sensibility and the imagination.
But when it is read at a later age, and with a maturer judgement,
it is seen that the elementary truths which it contains are expounded
in a manner which is very profound and sublime, and at the same
time with great sobriety. It was dictated by the Saint when she
was in ecstasy. Her teaching is in complete harmony with that of
St. Thomas and with that of St. John of the Cross. No one has
ever remarked any opposition between St. Catherine of Siena and
the Angelic Doctor ; nor do we see any that may be observed
between her and the author of the *Dark Night*.

[1] ix, 32.   [2] xviii, 2.   [3] Luke xxii, 31.

thy faith fail not; and thou, being once converted, confirm thy brethren.' This is a reference to the second conversion of Peter, which will take place at the end of the Passion, immediately after his denial.

It is to the second conversion that the greater part of this book will be devoted.

The
Three Conversions
in the
Spiritual Life

CHAPTER I

The Life of Grace and the Importance Of The First Conversion

THE interior life is for all the one thing necessary. It ought to be constantly developing in our souls; more so than what we call our intellectual life, more so than our scientific, artistic or literary life. The interior life is lived in the depths of the soul; it is the life of the whole man, not merely of one or other of his faculties. And our intellectual life would gain immeasurably by appreciating this; it would receive an inestimable advantage if, instead of attempting to supplant the spiritual life, it recognized its necessity and importance, and welcomed its beneficial influence —the influence of the theological virtues and the gifts of the Holy Ghost. How deeply important our subject is may be seen in the very words we have used : Intellectuality and Spirituality. And it is important to us not only as individuals, but also in our social relations; for it is evident that we can exert no real or profound influence upon our fellow-men unless we live a truly interior life ourselves.

The necessity of the interior life.

The pressing need of devoting ourselves to the

1

consideration of the one thing necessary is especially manifest in these days of general chaos and unrest, when so many men and nations, neglecting their true destiny, give themselves up entirely to acquiring earthly possessions, failing to realize how inferior these are to the everlasting riches of the spirit.

And yet St. Augustine's saying is so clearly true, that 'material goods, unlike those of the spirit, cannot belong wholly and simultaneously to more than one person.'[1] The same house, the same land, cannot belong completely to several people at once, nor the same territory to several nations. And herein lies the reason of that unhappy conflict of interests which arises from the feverish quest of these earthly possessions.

On the other hand, as St. Augustine often reminds us, the same spiritual treasure can belong in its entirety to all men, and at the same time to each, without any disturbance of peace between them. Indeed, the more there are to enjoy them in common the more completely do we possess them. The same truth, the same virtue, the same God, can belong to us all in like manner, and yet none of us embarrasses his fellow-possessors. Such are the inexhaustible riches of the spirit that they can be the property of all and yet satisfy the desires of each. Indeed, only then do we possess a truth completely when we teach it to others, when we make others share our contemplation; only then do we truly love a virtue when we wish others to love it also; only then do we wholly love God when we desire to make Him loved by all. Give money away, or spend it, and it is no longer yours. But give God to others, and you possess Him more fully for yourself. We may go even further and say that, if we desired only one

[1] St. Thomas often quotes this Augustinian thought: cf. I-IIae, Q. xxviii, art. 4, ad 2; III, Q. xxiii, art. 1, ad 3.

soul to be deprived of Him, if we excluded only one soul—even the soul of one who persecutes and calumniates us—from our own love, then God Himself would be lost to us.

This truth, so simple and yet so sublime, gives rise to an illuminating principle: it is that whereas material goods, the more they are sought for their own sake, tend to cause disunion among men, spiritual goods unite men more closely in proportion as they are more greatly loved. This principle helps us to appreciate how necessary is the interior life; and, incidentally, it virtually contains the solution of the social question and of the economic crisis which afflicts the world to-day. The Gospel puts it very simply: ' Seek ye first the kingdom of God and his justice, and all these things shall be added unto you.' If the world to-day is on its death-bed, it is because it has lost sight of a fundamental truth which for every Christian is elementary.

The profoundest truths of all, and the most vital, are in fact those elementary verities which, through long meditation and deep thought, have become the norm of our lives; those truths, in other words, which are the object of our habitual contemplation.

God is now showing men what a great mistake they make when they try to do without Him, when they regard earthly enjoyment as their highest good, and thus reverse the whole scale of values, or, as the ancient philosophers put it, the subordination of ends. As though in the hope of compensating for the poor quality of earthly goods, men are striving to increase their quantity; they are trying to produce as much as possible in the order of material enjoyment. They are constructing machinery with the object of increasing production at a greater profit. This is the ultimate objective. But what is the consequence?

The surplus cannot be disposed of ; it is wasted, and unemployment is the result. The worker starves in enforced idleness while others die of surfeit. The present state of the world is called a crisis. But in fact it is more than a crisis ; it is a condition of affairs which, if men only had eyes to see, ought to be revealing ; it ought to show men that they have sought their last end where it is not to be found, in earthly enjoyment—instead of God. They are seeking happiness in an abundance of material possessions which are incapable of giving it ; possessions which sow discord among those that seek them, and a greater discord according as they are sought with greater avidity.

Do what you will with these material goods : share them out equally, make them the common property of all. It will be no remedy for the evil ; for, so long as earthly possessions retain their nature and man retains the nature which is his, he will never find his happiness in them. The remedy is this, and this only : to consider the *one thing necessary*, and to ask God to give us *saints who live only on this thought*, saints who will give the world the spirit that it needs. God has always sent us saints in troubled times. We need them especially to-day.

The principle of the interior life.

It is all the more important to recall the necessity and the true nature of the interior life, because the true conception of it, as given to us in the Gospel, in the Epistles of St. Paul and in the whole of Tradition, has been partially obscured by many false ideas. In particular it is evident that the notion of the interior life is radically corrupted in the Lutheran theory of justification or conversion. According to this theory the mortal sins of the convert are not positively blotted out by the infusion of the new life of grace and charity; they are simply covered over, veiled by faith in the Redeemer, and they cease to be imputed to the person who has committed them. There is no intrinsic justification, no interior renewal of the soul; a man is reputed just merely by the extrinsic imputation of the justice of Christ. According to this view, in order to be just in the eyes of God it is not necessary to possess that infused charity by which we love God supernaturally and our fellow-men for God's sake. Actually, according to this conception, however firmly the just man may believe in Christ the Redeemer, he remains in his sin, in his corruption or spiritual death.[1]

This grave misconception concerning our super-natural life, reducing it essentially to faith in Christ and excluding sanctifying grace, charity and meri-torious works, was destined to lead gradually to Naturalism; it was to result finally in considering as ' just ' the man who, whatever his beliefs, valued and practised those natural virtues which were known even to the pagan philosophers who lived before Christ.[2]

[1] Luther went so far as to say : ' *Pecca fortiter et crede firmius :* Sin mightily and believe more mightily still ; you will be saved.' Not that Luther intended thereby to exhort men to sin ; it was merely an emphatic way of saying that good works are useless for salvation—that faith in Christ alone suffices. He says, truly enough (*Works*, Weimar edition, XII, 559 (1523)), that ' if you believe, good works will follow necessarily from your faith.' But, as Maritain justly observes (*Notes sur Luther ;* appendix to the second edition of *Trois Réformateurs*), ' in his thought these good works follow from salutary faith as a sort of epiphenomenon.' Moreover, the charity which will follow this faith is the love of our neighbour rather than the love of God. And thus the notion of charity is degraded, emptied gradually of its supernatural and God-ward content and made equivalent to works of mercy. In any case, it remains true that for Luther a man is justified simply by faith in Christ, even though the sin is not blotted out by the infusion of charity, or the supernatural love of God.

[2] J. Maritain explains very clearly how Naturalism arises neces-sarily from the principles of Protestantism : ' According to the

In such an outlook, the question which is actually of the first importance does not even arise : Is man capable in his present state, without divine grace, of observing all the precepts of the natural law, including those that relate to God ? Is he able without grace to love God the sovereign Good, the author of our nature, and to love Him, not with a merely inoperative affection, but with a truly efficacious love, more than he loves himself and more than he loves anything else ? The early Protestants would have answered in the negative, as Catholic theologians have always done.[1] Liberal Protestantism, the offspring of Luther's theology, does not even ask the question ; because it does not admit the necessity of grace, the necessity of an infused supernatural life.

Lutheran theology, it is we ourselves, and only we ourselves, who lay hold of the mantle of Christ so that with it we may " cover all our shame." ' It is we who exercise this ' ability to jump from our own sin on to the justice of Christ, thus becoming as sure of possessing the holiness of Christ as we are of possessing our own bodies.' The Lutheran theory of justification by faith may be called a Pelagianism born of despair. In ultimate analysis it is man who is left to work out his own redemption by stimulating himself to a despairing confidence in Christ. Human nature has then only to cast aside, as a useless theological accessory, the mantle of a grace which means nothing to him, and to transfer its faith-confidence from Christ to itself—and there you have that admirable emancipated brute, whose unfailing and continuous progress is an object of wonder to the universe. In Luther and his doctrine we witness—on the spiritual and religious plane—the *advent of the Ego*.

' We say that it is so *in fact ;* it is the inevitable outcome of Luther's theology. But this does not prevent the same theology *in theory* from committing the contrary excess. . . . And so Luther tells us that salvation and faith are to such an extent the work of God and of Christ that these *alone* are active in the business of our redemption, without any co-operation on our part. . . . Luther's theology was to oscillate between these two solutions : in theory it is the first, apparently, that must prevail : Christ alone, without our co-operation, is the author of our salvation. But since it is psychologically impossible to suppress human activity, the second has inevitably prevailed *in fact*.' It is a matter of history that liberal Protestantism has issued in Naturalism.

[1] Cf. St. Thomas, I–IIæ, Q. cix, art. 3 : ' Homo in statu naturæ integræ dilectionem suiipsius referebat ad amorem Dei sicut ad finem, et similiter dilectionem aliarum rerum, et ita Deum diligebat

Nevertheless, the question still recurs under a more general form: Is man able, *without some help from on high*, to get beyond himself, and truly and efficaciously to love Truth and Goodness more than he loves himself?

Clearly, these problems are essentially connected with that of the nature of our interior life; for our interior life is nothing else than a knowledge of the True and a love of the Good; or better, a knowledge and love of God.

In order fully to appreciate the lofty conception which the Scriptures, and especially the Gospels, give us of the interior life, it would be necessary to study a theological treatise on justification and sanctifying grace. Nevertheless, we may here emphasize a fundamental truth of the Christian spiritual life, or of Christian mysticism, which has always been taught by the Catholic Church.

In the first place it is clear that according to the Scriptures the justification or conversion of the sinner does not merely cover his sins as with a mantle; it blots them out by the infusion of a new life. ' Have mercy on me, O God, according to thy great mercy,' so the Psalmist implores; ' and according to the multitude of thy tender mercies blot out my iniquity. Wash me yet more from my iniquity and cleanse me from my sin. . . . Thou shalt sprinkle me with hyssop and I shall be cleansed; thou shalt wash me and I shall be made whiter than snow. . . . Blot out all my iniquities. Create a clean heart in me, O God; and renew a right spirit within my bowels. Cast me not away from thy face, and take not

plus quam seipsum et super omnia. Sed in statu naturæ corruptæ homo ab hoc deficit secundum appetitum voluntatis rationalis, quæ propter corruptionem naturæ sequitur bonum privatum, nisi sanetur per gratiam Dei.' *Ibid.*, art. 4: ' In statu naturæ corruptæ, non potest homo implere omnia mandata divina sine gratia sanante.'

thy holy spirit from me. Restore unto me the joy of thy salvation, and strengthen me with a perfect spirit.'[1]

The Prophets use similar language. Thus God says, through the prophet Isaias : ' I am he that blot out thy iniquities for my own sake.'[2] And the same expression recurs throughout the Bible : God is not content merely to cover our sins ; He blots them out, He takes them away. And therefore, when John the Baptist sees Jesus coming towards him, he says : ' Behold the Lamb of God. Behold him who taketh away the sin of the world ! ' We find the same idea in St. John's first Epistle :[3] 'The blood of Jesus Christ . . . cleanseth us from all sin.' St. Paul writes, similarly, in his first Epistle to the Corinthians :[4] ' Not the effeminate nor the impure nor thieves nor covetous nor drunkards nor railers nor extortioners shall possess the kingdom of God. And such some of you were. But you are washed ; but you are sanctified ; but you are justified ; in the name of our Lord Jesus Christ and the Spirit of our God.'

If it were true that by conversion sins were only veiled, and not blotted out, it would follow that a man is at once both just and ungodly, both justified, and yet still in the state of sin. God would love the sinner as His friend, despite the corruption of his soul, which He is apparently incapable of healing. The Saviour would not have taken away the sins of the world if He had not delivered the just man from the servitude of sin. Again, for the Christian these truths are elementary ; the profound understanding of them, the continual and quasi-experimental living of them, is what we call the contemplation of the saints.

The blotting out and remission of sins thus described by the Scriptures can be effected only by

---

[1] Ps. l, 3–14.   [2] Isa. xliii, 25.   [3] i, 7.   [4] vi, 10.

the infusion of sanctifying grace and charity—which is the supernatural love of God and of men for God's sake. Ezechiel, speaking in the name of God, tells us that this is so : ' I will pour upon you clean water, and you shall be cleansed from all your filthiness ; and I will cleanse you from all your idols. And I will give you a new heart, and put a new spirit within you ; and I will take away the stony heart out of your flesh and will give you a heart of flesh. And I will put my spirit in the midst of you ; and I will cause you to walk in my commandments.'[1]

This pure water which regenerates is the water of grace, of which it is said in the Gospel of St. John :[2] ' Of his fulness we have all received ; and grace for grace.' ' By (our Lord Jesus Christ) we have received grace,' we read in the Epistle to the Romans ;[3] . . . ' the charity of God is poured forth in our hearts, by the Holy Ghost who is given to us ' ;[4] and in the Epistle to the Ephesians : ' To every one of us is given grace, according to the measure of the giving of Christ.'[5]

If it were otherwise, God's uncreated love for the man whom He converts would be merely an idle affection, and not an effective and operative love. But God's uncreated love for us, as St. Thomas shows, is a love which, far from presupposing in us any *lovableness*, actually produces that lovableness within us. His creative love gives and preserves in us our nature and our existence ; but his life-giving love gives and preserves in us the life of grace which makes us *lovable* in His eyes, and lovable not merely as His servants but as His sons. (I, Q. xx, art. 2).

Sanctifying grace, the principle of our interior life, makes us truly the children of God because it

[1] xxxvi, 25.   [2] i, 16.   [3] i, 5.   [4] v, 5.   [5] iv, 7.

makes us partakers of His nature. We cannot be sons of God by nature, as the Word is; but we are truly sons of God by grace and by adoption. And whereas a man who adopts a child brings about no interior change in him, but simply declares him his heir, God, when He loves us as adoptive sons, transforms us inwardly, giving us a share in His own intimate divine life.

Hence we read in the Gospel of St. John :[1] ' (The Word) came unto his own, and his own received him not. But as many as received him, to them he gave the power to be made the sons of God, to them that believe in his name. Who are born, not of blood, nor of the will of the flesh, nor of the will of man, but of God.' And our Lord Himself said to Nicodemus :[2] ' Amen, amen, I say to thee, unless a man be born again of water and the Holy Ghost, he cannot enter into the kingdom of God. That which is born of the flesh is flesh ; and that which is born of the Spirit is spirit. Wonder not that I said to thee : You must be born again.'

St. John himself, moreover, writes in his first Epistle :[3] ' Whosoever is born of God committeth not sin ; for God's seed abideth in him. And he cannot sin because he is born of God.' In other words, the seed of God, which is grace—accompanied by charity, or the love of God—cannot exist together with mortal sin which turns a man away from God ; and, though it can exist together with venial sin, of which St. John had spoken earlier,[4] yet grace is not the source of venial sins ; on the contrary, it makes them gradually disappear.

Still clearer, if possible, is the language of St. Peter, who writes :[5] ' By (Christ) he hath given us most great and precious promises, that by these you may be made partakers of the divine nature ' ; and

[1] i, 11-13.   [2] John iii, 5.   [3] iii, 9.   [4] i, 8.   [5] 2 Pet. i, 4.

St. James[1] thus expresses the same idea: 'Every best gift and every perfect gift is from above, coming down from the Father of lights, with whom there is no change nor shadow of alteration. For of his own will hath he begotten us by the word of truth, that we might be some beginning of his creature.'

Truly sanctifying grace is a real and formal participation of the divine nature, for it is the principle of operations which are specifically divine. When in heaven it has reached its full development, and can no longer be lost, it will be the source of operations which will have absolutely the same formal object as the eternal and uncreated operations of God's own inner life; it will make us able to see Him immediately as He sees Himself, and to love Him as He loves Himself: 'Dearly beloved,' says St. John,[2] 'we are now the sons of God; and it hath not yet appeared what we shall be. We know that when it shall appear we shall be like to him, for we shall see him as he is.'

This is what shows us, better than anything else, in what the true nature of sanctifying grace, the true nature of our interior life, consists. We cannot emphasize it too much. It is one of the most consoling truths of our faith; it is one of those vital truths which serve best to encourage us in the midst of the trials of our life on earth.

The beginning of eternal life.

To understand what our interior life is in itself and in its various phases, we must consider it not merely in its seed, but in its full and complete development. Now, if we ask the Gospel what our interior life is, it tells us that the life of grace, given to us in Baptism and nourished by the Eucharist, is the seed or germ of eternal life.

[1] i, 17.   [2] 1 John iii, 2.

According to St. Matthew's account of the Sermon on the Mount, preached by Christ at the beginning of His ministry, our Lord says to His hearers (and it is the burden of the whole of His discourse): ' Be ye perfect as your heavenly Father is perfect.' He does not say : ' Be ye as perfect as the angels,' but ' as your heavenly Father is perfect.'[1] It follows, therefore, that Christ brings to men a principle of life which is a participation of the very life of God. Immeasurably above the various kingdoms of nature : the mineral kingdom, the vegetable, the animal kingdom, and even above the kingdom of man and above the natural activity of the angels, is the life of the kingdom of God. And this life in its full development is called, not the future life—of which even the better among the pre-Christian philosophers spoke—but *eternal life ;* a life measured, like that of God, not by future time, but by the one instant of motionless eternity.

The future life of which the philosophers speak is a natural life, similar almost to the life of the angels ; whereas eternal life, of which the Gospel speaks, is essentially supernatural, as much for the angels as for us. It is not merely superhuman, it is super-angelic, truly divine. It consists in seeing God immediately as He sees Himself, and in loving Him as He loves Himself. This is the reason why our Lord can say to you : ' Be ye perfect as your heavenly Father is perfect ' ; because you have received a participation in His inner life.

While the Old Testament speaks of eternal life only in figure, under the symbol of the Promised Land, the New Testament, and especially the Gospel of St. John, speaks of it continually ; and from that time forth it has become almost impossible to conclude a sermon without mentioning eternal life, as that

[1] Matt. v, 48.

supreme beatitude to which we are called and
destined.

But the Gospels, and especially the Gospel of
St. John, tell us more about grace ; we are told that
grace is eternal life already begun.

In the fourth Gospel our Lord is recorded as
saying no fewer than six times : ' He that believeth
in me hath eternal life.'[1] And it is not only in the
future that he will have it, if he perseveres ; in a
sense he possesses it already : ' He that eateth my
flesh and drinketh my blood hath eternal life, and I
will raise him up in the last day.'[2] What is the
meaning of these words ? Our Lord explains them
later : ' Amen, amen, I say to you : If any man keep
my word he shall not see death for ever. The Jews
therefore said : Now we know that thou hast a devil.
Abraham is dead, and the prophets ; and thou
sayest : If any man keep my word he shall not taste
death for ever. . . . Whom dost thou make thyself ? '
It was then that Jesus said : ' Before Abraham was,
I am.'[3]

What, then, does our Lord mean when He says :
' He that believeth in me hath eternal life ' ? He
means : He that believes in Me with a living faith,
that is, with a faith which is united with charity,
with the love of God and the love of his neighbour,
possesses eternal life already begun. In other words :
He who believes in Me has within himself in germ a
supernatural life which is fundamentally the same as
eternal life. Our spiritual progress cannot tend in the
direction of the life of eternity unless it presupposes
the seed of it already existing in us, a seed of the same
nature as the life towards which we are tending. In
the natural order, the germ which is contained in the
acorn could never grow into an oak tree unless it

[1] John iii, 36 ; v, 24, 39 ; vi, 40, 47, 55.   [2] vi, 55.
[3] viii, 51-58.

were of the same nature as the oak, if it did not contain the life of the oak in a latent state. The little child, likewise, could never become a man if it had not a rational soul, if reason were not already latent within it. In the same way, a Christian on earth could never become one of the blessed in heaven unless he had already received the divine life in Baptism.

And just as it is impossible to know the nature of the germ enclosed within the acorn unless we study it in its perfect state in the oak tree, so we cannot know the life of grace unless we consider it in its ultimate development, in that glory which is the consummation of grace. ' Grace,' says the whole of Tradition, ' is the seed of glory.'

Fundamentally, it is always the same supernatural life, the same sanctifying grace and the same charity, but with two differences. Here on earth we know God supernaturally, but not in the clearness of vision ; we know Him in the obscurity of faith. Moreover, while we hope one day to possess Him finally and definitively, here on earth it is always possible for us to lose Him by a mortal sin. But, in spite of these two differences, relating to faith and hope, it is the same life, the same sanctifying grace, and the same charity. And so our Lord said to the Samaritan woman : ' If thou didst know the gift of God and who he is that saith to thee : Give me to drink ; thou perhaps wouldst have asked of him, and he would have given thee living water. . . . He that shall drink of the water that I will give him shall not thirst for ever. But the water that I will give him shall become in him a fountain of water springing up into life everlasting.'[1] And in the Temple, on the last day of the feast of Tabernacles, Jesus stood and said in a loud voice, not merely for the benefit of privileged souls, but for

[1] John iv, 10–14.

all : ' If any man thirst let him come to me and drink. He that believeth in me . . . out of his belly shall flow rivers of living water.'[1] ' Now this he said,' adds St. John, ' of the Spirit which they should receive who believed in him.' And in fact the Holy Ghost is called *fons vivus, fons vitæ* : the living fountain, the fountain of life.

Again Jesus says : ' If any one love me he will keep my word (faith alone, then, is not enough), and my Father will love him, and we will come to him and will make our abode with him.'[2] Who will come ? Not only grace, God's created gift, but the divine Persons will come : the Father and the Son, and also the promised Holy Spirit. Thus the Holy Trinity dwells in us, in the obscurity of faith, in very much the same way as It dwells in the souls of the saints in heaven who see It face to face. ' He that abideth in charity abideth in God, and God in him.'[3]

It is much more wonderful than any miracle, this supernatural life. A miracle is an exercise of the divine omnipotence by which God signifies that one of His servants speaks in His name, or that he is of eminent sanctity. But even the raising of the dead to life, the miracle by which a corpse is reanimated with its natural life, is almost nothing in comparison with the resurrection of a soul, which has been lying spiritually dead in sin and has now been raised to the essentially supernatural life of grace.

Grace, then, is eternal life already begun within us ; and this is why Christ says : ' The kingdom of God cometh not with observation. Neither shall they say : Behold here or behold there. For lo, the kingdom of God is within you.'[4] It is there, hidden within you, like the grain of mustard seed, like the leaven which will cause the whole of the meal to

---

[1] John vii, 37.   [2] xiv, 23.   [3] I John iv, 16.
[4] Luke xvii, 20.

rise, like the treasure hidden in a field, like the source from which gushes a river of water that will never fail. ' We know,' says St. John, ' that we have passed from death to life, because we love the brethren ' ;[1] and ' these things I write to you that you may know that you have eternal life, you that believe in the name of the Son of God.'[2] And Christ, His beloved master, had said: ' This is eternal life: that they may know thee, the only true God, and Jesus Christ whom thou hast sent.'[3]

St. Thomas expresses this doctrine in the brief statement: ' *Gratia nihil aliud est quam quædam inchoatio gloriæ in nobis* ' : Grace is nothing else but a certain beginning of glory within us.'[4] And Bossuet says the same thing: ' Eternal life in its beginnings consists in knowing God by faith (united with charity) ; in its consummation eternal life consists in seeing God face to face, unveiled. Jesus Christ gives us both the one and the other, because He has merited it for us and because He is the source of it in all the members to which He gives life.'[5]

And therefore the Liturgy tells us, in the Preface used for the Mass of the Dead: ' *Tuis enim fidelibus, Domine, vita mutatur, non tollitur* ' : ' From them that believe in thee, O Lord, life is not taken away ; it is changed and transformed.'

The importance of true conversion.

We are thus able to appreciate something of the importance of true conversion, by which a man passes from the state of mortal sin to the state of grace. In the former state his energies were dissipated

---

[1] 1 John iii, 14.   [2] v, 13.   [3] John xvii, 3.
[4] II–IIæ, Q. xxiv, art. 3 ; I–IIæ, Q. lxix, art. 2 ; *De Ver.*, Q. xiv, art. 2.
[5] *Méditations sur l'Evangile*, II, 37th day ; *in Joan.*, xvii, 3.

and he was indifferent in regard to God; now he loves God more than he loves himself, more than he loves anything else; at any rate he esteems God beyond all earthly things, even though his love of God may not be free from all selfish motives. The state of sin was a state of spiritual death; a state in which, more or less consciously, he made himself the centre of all his activities and the end of all his desires; in which he was actually the slave of everything, the slave of his passions, of the spirit of the world, of the spirit of evil. The state of grace, on the other hand, is a state of life in which man begins seriously to tend beyond himself and to make God the centre of his activities, loving God more than himself. The state of grace is entrance into the kingdom of God, where the docile soul begins to reign with God over its own passions, over the spirit of the world and the spirit of evil.

We may well understand, therefore, how St. Thomas could write: '*Bonum gratiæ unius majus est quam bonum naturæ totius universi*': The lowest degree of grace in a soul, for example in that of a small child after its baptism, is of greater value than the natural goodness of the whole universe. This grace alone is worth more than all created natures together, including even the angelic natures. For the angels, too, stood in need, not of redemption, but of the gratuitous gift of grace in order to tend to the supernatural beatitude to which God called them. St. Augustine says that when God created the nature of the angels He also gave them the gift of grace: '*Simul in eis condens naturam et largiens gratiam*';[1] and he maintains that ' the justification of the ungodly is something greater than the creation of heaven and earth, greater even than the creation of the angels.'[2]

St. Thomas adds: ' The justification of the sinner

[1] *De civ. Dei*, lib. IV, c. 9.   [2] *In Joan.*, tract. 92, c. xiv, 12.

is proportionately more precious than the glorification of the just ; because the gift of grace more greatly transcends the state of the sinner, who is deserving of punishment, than the gift of glory transcends the state of the just man, who, by reason of his justification, is worthy of the gift of glory.'[1] There is a much greater distance between the nature of man, or even between the nature of the highest of the angels, and grace, than there is between grace itself and glory. No created nature, however perfect, is the germ of grace, whereas grace is indeed the germ or the seed of eternal life, *semen gloriæ*. Hence when a sinner is absolved in the confessional, an event occurs which is proportionately of greater importance than the entrance of a just soul into heaven.

This doctrine is expressed by Pascal in one of the finest pages of his *Pensées*, a page which summarises the teaching of St. Augustine and St. Thomas on this point : ' The infinite distance which separates bodies from spirits is a symbol of the infinitely more infinite distance which separates spirits from charity, for charity is supernatural.[2] The whole of the material creation together, the firmament, the stars, the earth and its kingdoms, is inferior to the least of the spirits ; for he knows all this and he knows himself, whereas bodies know nothing. All bodies together, and all spirits together, and all that they can produce, are of less value than the smallest act of charity, because this is of an infinitely higher order. From all bodies together it would be impossible to extract a single thought, because a thought is of a higher order than

[1] I–IIæ, Q. cxiii, art. 9.

[2] In reality there is a greater distance between any created nature, even the angelic nature, and the inner life of God, of which charity is a participation, than there is between bodies and created spirits. All creatures, even the highest, are at an infinite distance from God, and in this sense are equally below Him.

they. From all bodies and all spirits together it would be impossible to extract one single act of true charity, because an act of charity is of the supernatural order.'[1]

Luther erred fundamentally, therefore, when he tried to explain justification, not by the infusion of a grace and charity which remit sin, but merely by faith in Christ, without works and without love; making it consist simply in the extrinsic imputation of the merits of Christ, an imputation which covers sins without destroying them, and thus leaves the sinner in his filth and corruption. According to his view there was no regeneration of the will by the supernatural love of God and men. We have seen, on the contrary, what is the teaching of the Scriptures and of Tradition. Faith and the extrinsic imputation of the justice of Christ are not sufficient for the justification or conversion of the sinner. He must be willing, in addition, to observe the commandments, above all the two great commandments of the love of God and the love of one's neighbour: ' If any one love me he will keep my word, and my Father will love him, and we will come to him and make our abode with him.'[2] ' He that abideth in charity abideth in God, and God in him.'[3]

According to the true teaching of Christ we are in an order far transcending natural morality. Our unaided reason tells us that it is our duty to love God, *the author of our nature,* and to love Him effectively, that is, by observing His commandments. But even this natural duty we are unable to fulfil without the help of God's grace, so weakened are our wills in consequence of original sin. Still less are we able by our natural powers alone to love God, *the author of grace ;* for this love is of an essentially supernatural order, as supernatural for the angels as it is for us.

[1] *Pensées* (ed. Havet), p. 269.   [2] John xiv, 23.   [3] 1 John iv, 16.

Such is the supernatural life which we received in Baptism; and this is what constitutes our interior life.

This beginning of eternal life, as we have called it, is a complete *spiritual organism*, which has to grow and develop until we enter heaven. The root principle of this undying organism is *sanctifying grace*, received in the very essence of the soul; and this grace would last for ever, were it not that sin, a radical disorder in the soul, sometimes destroys it.[1] From sanctifying grace, which is the germ of glory, proceed the infused virtues. First, the *theological virtues*, the greatest of which, charity, is destined to last for ever: 'Charity never falleth away,' says St. Paul, . . . 'Now there remain faith, hope and charity, these three; but the greatest of these is charity.'[2] Charity will remain for ever, after faith has disappeared to make room for vision; after hope has been displaced by the everlasting possession of God, seen face to face.

In addition to the theological virtues there are also the *infused moral virtues*, which perfect man in his use of the means of salvation, just as the former dispose him rightly in regard to his end. The infused moral virtues are like so many functions admirably adapted one to another, infinitely surpassing in perfection those of our physical organism; they are called: prudence, justice, fortitude and temperance . . . together with the other virtues which are associated with them.

Finally, in order to supply the deficiencies of these virtues which, in the twilight of faith and under the direction of prudence, still act in too human a fashion, we are given the *seven gifts of the Holy Ghost*, who dwells in us. These are like the sails on a ship;

[1] Cf. I-IIæ, Q. lxxxvii, art. 3.   [2] I Cor. xiii, 8, 13.

they dispose us to receive obediently and promptly the breathing that comes from on high, the special inspirations of God ; inspirations which enable us to act, no longer in merely human fashion, but divinely, with that alacrity which we need in order to run in the way of God, undismayed by any obstacles.

All these infused virtues and gifts grow with sanctifying grace and charity, says St. Thomas ;[1] they increase together just as the five fingers of the hand, or the organs of our body, develop simultaneously. Thus it is inconceivable that a soul should possess a high degree of charity without possessing at the same time *a proportionate degree of the gift of wisdom ;* whether this exist under a definitely contemplative form, or in a practical guise, more directly adapted to action. The wisdom of a St. Vincent de Paul is unlike that of a St. Augustine ; but the one and the other are equally infused.

In this way the whole of the spiritual organism develops simultaneously, though it may manifest its activity under various forms. And, from this point of view, since the infused contemplation of the mysteries of faith is an act of the gifts of the Holy Ghost, an act which disposes the soul to the beatific vision, must we not admit that such contemplation is in the normal way of sanctity ?—We merely mention the question here, without insisting further upon it.[2]

Let us now examine more closely the full development of our eternal life in heaven, in order that we may better appreciate the value of that sanctifying grace which is its beginning. In particular let us compare it with what would have been our beatitude

---

[1] I–IIæ, Q. lxvi, art. 2.
[2] We have treated it fully elsewhere : *Perfection chrétienne et contemplation*, t. II, pp. 430–462 ; see also note below, p. 105.

and our reward if we had been created in a purely natural state.

If we had been created in a state of pure nature, with a spiritual and immortal soul, but without the life of grace, even then our intellect would have been made for the knowledge of the True and our will for the love of the Good. Our end would have been to know God, the Sovereign Good, the author of our nature, and to love Him above all things. But we should have known Him only in the reflection of His goodness in creatures, in the same way as the greatest among the pagan philosophers knew Him, though our knowledge would have been more certain than theirs, and free from any admixture of error. God would have been for us the First Cause and the Supreme Intelligence that orders all the things of creation.

We should have loved Him as the author of our nature, with that love which a subject has for his superior. It would not have been a love of friendship, but rather a sentiment compounded of admiration, respect and gratitude, yet lacking that happy and simple familiarity which rejoices the hearts of the children of God. We should have been God's servants, but not His children.

This natural end is already a sublime destiny. It could never bring satiety, just as the eye never tires of contemplating the blue vault of heaven. Moreover, it is a spiritual end, and therefore, unlike material goods, can be possessed at once by all and by each, without possession on the part of one being prejudicial to possession on the part of another, and thus without causing jealousy or discord.

But this abstract and mediate knowledge of God would have left many obscurities in the human mind, especially as regards the mutual compatibility of the divine perfections. We should forever have remained at the stage of counting singly and enumerating these absolute perfections ; we should forever have wondered how it was possible to reconcile the almighty goodness of God with His permission that evil should exist ; an evil, too, which is sometimes so great as to disconcert the human mind. We should have asked ourselves, moreover, how His infinite mercy could be truly consistent with His infinite justice. Even though we enjoyed this natural beatitude, we should still be urged to say : ' If only I could *see this God*, who is the source of all truth and goodness ; if I could see Him as He sees Himself ! '

What the most brilliant of human minds, what even the intelligence of the angels could never have discovered, divine Revelation has disclosed to us. Revelation tells us that our last end is essentially supernatural and that it consists *in seeing God immediately, face to face, as He is : sicuti est* ' (God) has predestinated (us) to be made conformable to the image of his Son ; that he might be the firstborn among many brethren.'[1] ' Eye hath not seen, nor ear heard, neither hath it entered into the heart of man, what things God hath prepared for them that love him.'[2]

We are destined to see God, not merely in the mirror of creatures, however perfect these may be, but to see Him immediately, without the intermediary of any creature, and even without the medium of any created idea ; for no created idea, however perfect, could ever represent as He really is One who is Thought itself, infinite Truth, the eternally subsistent brightness of intelligence and the living flame of measureless Love.

We are destined to see all the divine perfections concentrated and intimately united in their common

[1] Rom. viii, 29.   [2] 1 Cor. ii, 9.

source : Deity. We are destined to see how the tenderest Mercy and the most inexorable Justice proceed from the one Love which is infinitely generous and infinitely holy ; how this Love, even in its freest choice, is identically one with pure Wisdom, how there is nothing in the divine Love which is not wise, nothing in the divine Wisdom which is not synonymous with Love. We are destined to contemplate the eminent simplicity of God, His absolute purity and sanctity ; to see the infinite fecundity of the divine nature in the procession of the Three Persons : to contemplate the eternal generation of the Word, the ' brightness of (the Father's) glory and the figure of his substance,'[1] to see the ineffable breathing of the Holy Spirit, the issue of the common Love of the Father and the Son, which unites them in the most complete outpouring of themselves. The Good tends naturally to diffuse itself, and the greater the Good the more abundant and intimate is its self-giving.

None can tell the joy and the love which this vision will produce in us, a love of God so pure and so strong that nothing will ever be able to destroy or in the slightest degree to diminish it.

In no way, therefore, can we express more clearly the preciousness of sanctifying grace, or of the true interior life, than by saying that it is a beginning of eternal life. Here on earth we know God only by faith, and, while we hope one day to possess Him, we are able, unfortunately, to lose Him by sin. But, apart from these two differences, it is fundamentally the same life, the same sanctifying grace and the same charity, which is to last through all eternity.

This is the fundamental truth of Christian spirituality. Consequently our interior life must be a life

[1] Heb. i, 3.

of *humility*, for we must remember always that the principle of that life, sanctifying grace, is a gratuitous gift, and that we need an actual grace for the slightest salutary act, for the shortest step forward in the way of salvation. It must be also a life of *mortification*; as St. Paul says, we must be ' always bearing about in our body the mortification of Jesus, that the life also of Jesus may be made manifest in our bodies ' ;[1] that is to say: we must daily more and more die to sin and to the relics that sin leaves in us, so that God may reign more completely in us, even to the depth of the soul. But, above all, our interior life must be a life of *faith, hope, charity, and union with God* by unceasing prayer; it is above all the life of the three theological virtues and of the gifts of the Holy Ghost which accompany them: the gifts of wisdom, understanding, knowledge, piety, counsel, fortitude and fear of the Lord. In this way we shall enter into the mysteries of faith and relish them more and more. In other words, our whole interior life tends towards the supernatural contemplation of the mysteries of the inner life of God and of the Incarnation and Redemption; it tends, above all, towards a more intimate union with God, a preliminary to that union with Him, ever actual and perpetual, which will be the consummation of eternal life.

The three periods of the spiritual life.

If such is the life of grace, if such is the spiritual organism of the infused virtues and the gifts, it is not surprising to find that the development of the interior life has often been compared to the three periods or stages of physical life: childhood, youth, and manhood. St. Thomas himself has indicated this analogy: and it is an analogy which is worth

[1] 2 Cor. iv, 10.

pursuing, particular attention being paid to the transition from one period to the other.

It is generally admitted that childhood lasts until the age of puberty, about fourteen; though early childhood, or infancy, ceases at the dawn of reason, about the age of seven. Youth, or adolescence, lasts from the age of fourteen to twenty. Then follows manhood, in which we may distinguish the period which precedes full maturity, about the age of thirty-five, and that which follows it, before the decline of old age sets in.

A man's mentality changes with the development of the organism : the activity of the child, it has been said, is not that of a man in miniature, or of a fatigued adult ; the dominant element in childhood is different. The child has as yet no discernment, it is unable to organize in a rational manner ; it follows the lead of the imagination and the impulses of sense. And even when its reason begins to awaken it still remains to a great extent dependent upon the senses. So, for example, a child asked me one day : ' What are you lecturing on this year ? ' ' On man,' I replied.

' On what man ? ' was the next inquiry. The child's intelligence was as yet unable to grasp the abstract and universal idea of man as such.

Most important to be noticed, for the purposes of our present subject, is the transition from childhood to adolescence and from youth to manhood.

The period of puberty, which is the end of childhood, about the age of fourteen, is characterized by a transformation which is not only organic but also psychological, intellectual and moral. The youth is no longer content to follow his imagination, as the child was ; he begins to reflect on the things of human life, on the need to prepare himself for some career or occupation in the future. He has no longer the child's attitude towards family, social and religious matters ; his moral personality begins to take shape, and he acquires the sense of honour and of good repute. Or else, on the contrary, if he passes unsuccessfully through this difficult period, he deteriorates and follows evil courses. The law of nature so ordains that the transition from childhood to youth must follow a normal development ; otherwise the subject will assume a positive bias to evil, or else he will remain a half-wit, perhaps even a complete idiot, for the rest of his life. 'He who makes no progress loses ground.'

It is at this point that the analogy becomes illuminating for the spiritual life. We shall see that the beginner who fails to become a proficient, either turns to sin or else presents an example of arrested spiritual development. Here, too, it is true that 'he who makes no progress loses ground,' as the Fathers of the Church have so often pointed out.

Let us pursue the analogy further. If the physical and moral crisis of puberty is a difficult transition, the same is to be said of another crisis, which we may call the crisis of the first freedom, and which occurs at the stage where the youth enters manhood, about the age of twenty. The young man, having now reached his complete physical development, has to begin to take his place in social life. It will soon be time for him to marry and to become an educator in his turn, unless he has received from God a higher vocation still. Many fail to surmount this crisis of the first freedom, and, like the prodigal son, depart from their father's house and confuse liberty with licence. Here again the law ordains that the transition must be made normally ; otherwise the young man either takes the wrong road, or else his development is arrested and he becomes one of those of whom it is said : ' He will be a child for the whole of his life.'

The true adult is not merely a young man grown a little older. He has a new mentality ; he is pre-occupied with wider questions, questions to which the youth does not yet advert. He understands the younger generation, but the younger generation does not understand him ; conversation between them on certain subjects, except of a very superficial kind, is impossible.

There is a somewhat similar relation, in the spiritual life, between the proficient and the perfect. He who is perfect understands the earlier stages through which he has himself already passed ; but he cannot expect to be understood by those who are still passing through them.

The important thing to be noticed is that, just as there is the crisis of puberty, more or less manifest and more or less successfully surpassed, between childhood and adolescence, so in the spiritual life there is an analogous crisis for the transition from the purgative life of beginners to the illuminative life of proficients. This crisis has been described by several great spiritual writers, in particular by Tauler[1] and especially by St. John of the Cross, under the name of the *passive purgation of the senses*,[2] and by Père Lallemant, S.J.,[3] and several others under the name of the *second conversion*.

Moreover, just as the youth has to pass through a second crisis, that of the first freedom, in order to reach manhood, so in the transition from the illumina-tive way of the proficients to the true life of union, there is a second spiritual crisis, mentioned by

---

[1] *Second Sermon for Lent.*
[2] *Dark Night*, Book I, ch. 9 and ch. 10.
[3] *Doctrine Spirituelle*, Pr. II, sect. ii, ch. 6, art. 2.

Tauler,[1] and described by St. John of the Cross under
the name of the *passive purgation of the spirit*.[2] This,
likewise, may be called a third conversion, or better,
a transformation of the soul.

None has better described these crises which mark
the transition from one spiritual period to another
than St. John of the Cross. It will be noticed that
they correspond to the two parts of the human soul,
the sensitive and the spiritual. They correspond
also to the nature of the divine seed, sanctifying
grace, that germ of eternal life which must ever
more and more animate all our faculties and inspire
all our actions, until the depth of the soul is purged
of all egoism and surrendered entirely to God.

St. John of the Cross, it is true, describes spiritual
progress as it appears especially in contemplatives,
and in the most generous among contemplatives, who
are striving to reach union with God by the most
direct way possible. He therefore shows us what are
the higher laws of the spiritual life at their maximum
of sublimity. But these laws apply in a lesser degree
also to many other souls who do not reach so high a
state of perfection, but are nevertheless making
devoted progress, and not looking back.

In the chapters which follow it will be our object to
show that, according to the traditional teaching,
beginners in the spiritual life must, after a certain
period, undergo a second conversion, similar to the
second conversion of the Apostles at the end of our
Lord's Passion, and that, still later, before entering
upon the life of perfect union, there must be a third
conversion or transformation of the soul, similar to
that which took place in the souls of the Apostles on
the day of Pentecost.

This distinction between the three periods or stages

---

[1] *Sermon for Monday in Passion Week.*
[2] *Dark Night*, Book II, ch. 1–13.

of the spiritual life is clearly of great importance, as those who are charged with the direction of souls well know. An old and experienced director who has himself reached the age of the perfect may have read but little of the writings of the mystics, and yet he will be able to answer well and readily the most delicate questions on the most sublime subjects; and he will answer in the words of the Scriptures, perhaps by quoting a passage from the Gospel of the day, without even suspecting for a moment how truly profound his answers are. On the other hand a young and inexperienced priest, himself only at the age of a beginner, will have little more than a book-knowledge and a verbal acquaintance with the spiritual life.

The question with which we are concerned is thus in the highest sense a *vital* question; and it is important that we should consider it from the traditional point of view. If we do so consider it, we shall see how true is the saying of the ancients, that ' in the way of God he who makes no progress loses ground '; and it will appear also that our interior life must, already here on earth, become the normal prelude to the beatific vision. In this deep sense our interior life is, as we have said, eternal life already begun: ' *inchoatio vitæ æternæ.*'[1] ' Amen, amen I say to you, he that believeth in me hath eternal life, and I will raise him up in the last day.'[2]

---

[1] II–IIæ, Q. xxiv, art. 3, ad 2; I–IIæ, Q. lxix, art. 2.
[2] John vi, 47–55.

CHAPTER II

The Second Conversion: Entrance into The Illuminative Way

WE have seen that, comparable with the two crises which mark the transition from childhood to youth and from youth to manhood, there are also in the spiritual life two crises, one by which proficients pass into the illuminative way, and another by which the perfect reach the state of union.

The first of these crises has been called a second conversion, and it is of this that we have now to speak.

The liturgy, especially at periods such as Advent and Lent, speaks often of the need of conversion, even for those who are leading a Christian life. Spiritual writers also refer often to this second conversion, necessary for the Christian who, though he has thought seriously of his salvation and made an effort to walk in the way of God, has nevertheless begun once more to follow the bent of his nature and to fall into a state of tepidity—like an engrafted plant reverting to its wild state. Some of these writers, such as the Blessed Henry Suso or Tauler, have insisted especially upon the necessity of this second conversion, a necessity which they have learned from their own experience. St. John of the Cross has profoundly pointed out that the entrance into the illuminative way is marked by a passive purgation of the senses, which is a second conversion, and that the entrance into the unitive way is preceded by a passive purgation of the spirit, a further and a deeper conversion affecting the soul in its most intimate

depths.   Among the writers of the Society of Jesus
we may quote Père Lallemant, who writes : ' Saints
and religious who reach perfection pass ordinarily
through two conversions : one by which they *devote
themselves to the service of God*, and another by which
they surrender themselves entirely to perfection.   We
find this in the case of the Apostles, first when our
Lord called them, and then when He sent the Holy
Ghost upon them ; we find it in the case of St.
Teresa, of her confessor, P. Alvarez, and of many
others.   This second conversion is not granted to all
religious, and it is due to their negligence.'[1]

This question is of the greatest interest for every
spiritual soul.   Among those who dealt with it before
St. John of the Cross we must count St. Catherine of
Siena, who touches upon the subject repeatedly in
her *Dialogue* and in her *Letters*.   Her treatment,
which is very realistic and practical, throws a great
light upon the teaching which is commonly received
in the Church.[2]

Following St. Catherine, we shall speak first of this
second conversion as it took place in the Apostles,
and then as it should take place in us ; we shall say
what defects render this conversion necessary, what
great motives ought to inspire it, and finally what
fruits it should produce in us.

The second conversion of the Apostles.

St. Catherine of Siena speaks explicitly of the
second conversion of the Apostles in the 63rd chapter
of her *Dialogue*.

---

[1] *La Doctrine Spirituelle*, Pr. II, sect. ii, ch. 6, art. 2.

[2] This is not an instance of a private revelation relating to some
future event or some new truth ; it is a more profound contemplation of a truth already revealed in the Gospel—a fulfilment
of the promise of Christ that the Holy Spirit would call to mind
whatsoever He had told to His Apostles (John xiv, 26).

Their first conversion had taken place when Jesus called them, with the words : ' I will make you fishers of men.' They followed our Lord, listened with admiration to His teaching, saw His miracles and took part in His ministry. Three of them saw Him transfigured on Thabor. All were present at the institution of the Eucharist, were ordained priests and received Holy Communion. But when the hour of the Passion arrived, an hour which Jesus had so often foretold, the Apostles abandoned their Master. Even Peter, though he loved his Master devotedly, went so far as to deny Him thrice. Our Lord had told Peter after the Supper, in words that recall the prologue of the Book of Job : ' Simon, Simon, behold Satan hath desired to have you, that he may sift you as wheat. But I have prayed for thee that thy faith fail not ; and thou being once converted confirm thy brethren.' To which Peter replied : ' Lord, I am ready to go with thee both into prison and to death.' But Jesus warned him : ' I say to thee, Peter, the cock shall not crow this day till thou thrice deniest that thou knowest me.'[1]

And, in fact, Peter fell ; he denied his Master, swearing that he did not know Him.

When did his second conversion begin ? Immediately after his triple denial, as we are told in the Gospel of St. Luke :[2] ' Immediately, as he was yet speaking, the cock crew. And the Lord turning, looked on Peter. And Peter remembered the word of the Lord, as he had said : Before the cock crow, thou shalt deny me thrice. And Peter going out, wept bitterly.' Under the glance of Jesus and the grace which accompanied it, Peter's repentance must have been deep indeed and must have been the beginning of a new life for him.

In connection with this second conversion of St.

---

[1] Luke xxii, 31–34.   [2] xxii, 60–62.

Peter it is well to recall the words of St. Thomas :[1]
' Even after a grave sin, if the soul has a sorrow which
is truly fervent and proportionate to the degree of
grace which it has lost, it will recover this same
degree of grace ; grace may even revive in the soul
in a higher degree, if the contrition is still more
fervent. Thus the soul has not to begin again
completely from the beginning, but it continues
from the point which it had reached at the moment
of the fall.' In the same way, the climber who falls
when he has reached half-way up the mountain-side,
rises immediately and continues his ascent from the
point at which he has fallen.[2]

Everything leads us to suppose that Peter's
repentance was so fervent that he not only recovered
the degree of grace which he possessed before, but
was raised to a higher degree of supernatural life.
Our Lord had allowed him to fall in this way in order
to cure him of his presumption, so that he might be
more humble and place his confidence in God and
not in himself.

St. Catherine writes in her *Dialogue* :[3] ' Peter . . .
after the sin of denying My Son, began to weep.
Yet his lamentations were imperfect, and remained
so until after the forty days, that is until after the
Ascension. (They remained imperfect in spite of

---

[1] III, Q. lxxxix, art. 2.

[2] The teaching of St. Thomas is quite clear : ' Contingit inten-
sionem motus pœnitentis quandoque proportionatum esse majori
gratiæ, quam fuerit illa a qua ceciderat per peccatum, quandoque
æquali, quandoque vero minori. Et ideo pœnitens quandoque
resurgit in majori gratia, quam prius habuerat, quandoque autem
in æquali, quandoque etiam in minori' (III, Q. lxxxix, art. 2).
Certain modern theologians think that it is possible to recover a
high degree of grace with an attrition which is barely sufficient.
St. Thomas and the ancient theologians do not admit this. And
in fact we find in human relationships that, after considerable
offence has been given, friendship will revive in the same degree
as it existed before only if there is, not merely regret, but regret
proportionate to the offence committed and to the greatness of the
previous friendship.

[3] Ch. 63.

the appearances of our Lord.) But when my Truth
returned to me, in His humanity, Peter and the
others concealed themselves in the house, awaiting
the coming of the Holy Spirit which my Truth had
promised them. They remained barred in through
fear, because the soul always fears until it arrives at
true love.' It was only at Pentecost that they were
truly transformed.

Yet even before the end of the Passion of Christ
there was clearly a second conversion in Peter and
the other Apostles, a conversion which was con-
solidated during the days that followed. After His
resurrection our Lord appeared to them several
times, enlightening them, as He did when He taught
the disciples of Emmaus the understanding of the
Scriptures; and in particular, after the miraculous
draught of fishes, He made Peter compensate for his
threefold denial by a threefold act of love. ' Simon,
son of John,' He says to him, ' lovest thou me more
than these? He saith to him: Yea, Lord, thou
knowest that I love thee. He saith to him: Feed
my lambs. He saith to him again: Simon, son of
John, lovest thou me. He saith to him: Yea, Lord,
thou knowest that I love thee. He saith to him:
Feed my lambs. He said to him the third time:
Simon, son of John, lovest thou me? Peter was
grieved because he said to him the third time:
Lovest thou me? And he said to him: Lord, thou
knowest all things, thou knowest that I love thee.
He said to him: Feed my sheep.' And then He
foretold in veiled terms the martyrdom that Peter
would undergo: ' When thou wast younger thou
didst gird thyself and didst walk where thou wouldst.
But when thou shalt be old, thou shalt stretch forth
thy hands and another shall gird thee and lead thee
whither thou wouldst not.'[1]

[1] John xxi, 15 seq.

The threefold act of love made reparation for the threefold denial. It was a consolidation of the second conversion, a measure of confirmation in grace before the transformation of Pentecost.

For St. John, too, there had been something special just before the death of Christ. John, like the other Apostles, had abandoned his Master when Judas arrived with his band of armed men ; but by an invisible and powerful grace Jesus drew the beloved disciple to the foot of the cross, and the second conversion of St. John took place when he heard the seven last words of the dying Saviour.

What our second conversion ought to be. The defects which render it necessary.

In the 60th and 63rd chapters of her *Dialogue,* St. Catherine shows that what happened in the case of the Apostles, our models formed immediately by the Saviour Himself, must happen, after a certain manner, in the case of each one of us. Indeed we may say that if even the Apostles stood in need of a second conversion, then still more do we. The Saint emphasizes especially the faults which make this second conversion necessary, in particular self-love. In varying degrees this egoism survives in all imperfect souls in spite of the state of grace, and it is the source of a multitude of venial sins, of habitual faults which become characteristic features of the soul, rendering necessary a veritable purging even in those who have, as it were, been present on Mount Thabor, or who have often partaken of the Eucharistic banquet, as the Apostles did at the Last Supper.

In her *Dialogue*[1] St. Catherine of Siena speaks of this self-love, describing it as ' the mercenary love

[1] Ch. 60.

of the imperfect,' of those who, without being conscious of it, serve God from self-interest, because they are attached to temporal or spiritual consolations, and who shed tears of self-pity when they are deprived of them.

It is a strange but not uncommon mixture of sincere love of God with an inordinate love of self.[1] The soul loves God more than itself, otherwise it would not be in the state of grace, it would not possess charity ; but it still loves itself with an inordinate love. It has not yet reached the stage of loving itself in God and for His sake. Such a state of soul is neither white nor black ; it is a light grey, in which there is more white than black. The soul is on the upward path, but it still has a tendency to slip downwards.

We read in this 60th chapter of the *Dialogue* (it is God who speaks) : ' Among those who have become My trusted servants there are some who serve Me with faith, without servile fear ; it is not the mere fear of punishment, but *love which attaches them to My service* (thus Peter before the Passion). But this love is still *imperfect,* because *what they seek in My service* (at any rate to a great extent) *is their own profit, their own satisfaction, or the pleasure that they find in Me.* The same imperfection is found in the love which they bear towards their neighbour. And do you know what shows the imperfection of their love ? It is that, as soon as they are deprived of the consolations which they find in Me, their love fails and can no longer survive. It becomes weak and gradually cools towards Me when, in order to

---

[1] According to St. Thomas this mixture is impossible in the angels, because they cannot sin venially. They are either very holy or very perverse. Either they love God perfectly, or else they turn away from Him completely by mortal sin. This is due to the vigour of their intelligence, which enters completely and definitively into the way it has taken (I–IIæ, Q. lxxxix, art. 4).

exercise them in virtue and to detach them from their imperfection, I withdraw spiritual consolations from them and send them difficulties and afflictions. I act in this way in order to bring them to perfection, to *teach them to know themselves*, to realize that they are nothing and that *of themselves they have no grace*.[1] Adversity should have the effect of making them seek refuge in Me, recognize Me as their benefactor, and become attached to Me by a true humility. . . .

' If they do not recognize their imperfection and desire to become perfect, it is impossible that they should not turn back.' This is what the Fathers have so often asserted : ' In the way of God he who makes no progress loses ground.' Just as the child who does not grow does not merely remain a child but becomes an idiot, so the beginner who does not enter upon the way of proficients when he ought to, does not merely remain a beginner, but becomes a stunted soul. It would seem, unhappily, that the great majority of souls do not belong to any of these three categories, of beginners, proficients or perfect, but rather to that of stunted souls ! At what stage are we ourselves ? This is often a very difficult question to answer, and it would perhaps be vain curiosity to inquire at what point we have arrived in our upward path ; but at least we must take care not to mistake the road, not to take a path that leads downwards.

It is important, therefore, to reach beyond the merely mercenary love, which often we unconsciously retain. We read in this same 60th chapter : ' It was with this imperfect love that Peter loved the good

---

[1] This is the quasi-experimental knowledge of the distinction between nature and grace, quite different from that which we have through speculative theology. It is not difficult to understand in abstract the difference between the two orders ; but to see it in concrete, and to perceive it almost continuously, supposes a spirit of faith which, in this degree, is found hardly in any but the Saints.

and gentle Jesus, my only-begotten Son, when he experienced the delights of sweet intimacy with Him (on Mount Thabor). But as soon as the time of tribulation came all his courage forsook him. Not only did he not have the strength to suffer for Him, but at the first threat of danger his loyalty was overcome by the most servile fear, and he denied Him three times, swearing that he did not know Him.'

St. Catherine of Siena, in the 63rd chapter of the same *Dialogue*, shows that the imperfect soul, which loves God with a love which is still mercenary, must do what Peter did after his denial. Not infrequently Providence allows us, too, at this stage to commit some very palpable fault, in order to humiliate us and cause us to take true measure of ourselves.

' Then,' says the Lord,[1] ' having recognized the grievousness of its sin and repented of it, the soul begins to weep, for fear of punishment ; then it rises to the consideration of my mercy, in which it finds satisfaction and comfort. But it is, I say, *still imperfect, and in order to draw it on to perfection* . . . *I withdraw from it,* not in grace but *in feeling*.[2] . . . This I do in order to humiliate that soul, and cause it to seek Me in truth . . . without thought of self and with lively faith and with hatred of its own sensuality.' And just as Peter compensated for his threefold denial by three acts of pure and devoted love, so the enlightened soul must do in like manner.

St. John of the Cross, following Tauler, gives us

---

[1] *Dialogue*, ch. 63.

[2] Thus our Lord deprived His disciples of His visible presence, saying to them : ' It is expedient to you that I go.' It was in fact expedient that they should be for some time deprived of the sight of His humanity, so that they might be elevated to a higher spiritual life, a life more independent of the senses, a life which would later, when made more vigorous, find expression in the sacrifice of an heroic martyrdom.

three signs which mark this second conversion : ' The soul finds no pleasure or consolation in the things of God, but it also fails to find it in any thing created. . . . The second sign . . . is that ordinarily the memory is centred upon God, with painful care and solicitude, thinking that it is not serving God, but backsliding, because it finds itself without sweetness in the things of God. . . . The third sign . . . is that the soul can no longer meditate or reflect in its sense of the imagination. . . . For God now begins to communicate Himself to it, no longer through sense, as He did aforetime, by means of reflections which joined and sundered its knowledge, but by an act of simple contemplation, to which neither the exterior nor the interior senses of the lower part of the soul can attain.'[1]

Progressives or proficients thus enter, according to St. John of the Cross, ' upon the road and way of the spirit, which . . . is called the way of illumination or of infused contemplation, wherewith God Himself feeds and refreshes the soul.'[2]

While St. Catherine of Siena does not give so exact an analysis, she insists particularly upon one of the signs of this state : *an experimental knowledge of our poverty* and profound imperfection ; a knowledge which is not precisely acquired, but granted by God, as it was granted to Peter when Jesus looked upon him immediately after his denial. At that moment Peter received a grace of enlightenment ; he remembered, and going out he wept bitterly.[3]

At the end of this same 63rd chapter of her *Dialogue* we find a passage of which St. John of the Cross later gives a full development : ' I withdraw from the soul,' says the Lord, ' so that it may see and know its defects, so that, feeling itself deprived of consolation and afflicted by pain, it may recognize its own

[1] *Dark Night*, Book I, ch. 9.   [2] *Ibid.*, ch. 14.   [3] Luke xxii, 61.

weakness, and learn how incapable it is of stability or perseverance, thus cutting down to the very root of spiritual self-love ; for this should be the end and purpose of all its self-knowledge, to rise above itself, mounting the throne of conscience, and not permitting the sentiment of imperfect love to turn again in its death-struggle, but, with correction and reproof, digging up the root of self-love, with the knife of self-hatred and the love of virtue.'[1]

In this same connection the Saint speaks of the many dangers that lie in wait for a soul that is moved only by a mercenary love, saying that souls which are imperfect desire to follow the Father alone, without passing by the way of Christ crucified, because they have no desire to suffer.[2]

The motives which must inspire the second conversion, and the fruits that derive therefrom.

The first motive is expressed in the greatest commandment, which knows no limits : ' Thou

---

[1] It is obvious that when the Saint speaks of ' self-hatred ' she has in mind the aversion which we must have for that self-love, or inordinate love of self, which is the source of all sin. Self-love, she tells us in chapter 122 of the *Dialogue*, is the cause of injustice towards God, towards one's neighbour, and towards oneself ; it destroys in the soul both the desire for the salvation of souls and the hunger for virtue ; it prevents the soul from reacting as it should against the most crying injustices, because of the inordinate fear of offending creatures that self-love entails. ' Self-love,' she says, ' has poisoned the whole world and the mystical body of the holy Church, and through self-love the garden of the Spouse has run to seed and given birth to putrid flowers.'

' Thou knowest,' God says to the Saint (ch. 51), ' that every evil is founded in self-love, and that self-love is a cloud that takes away the light of reason, which reason holds in itself the light of faith, and one is not lost without the other.' We find the same doctrine in St. Thomas : ' Inordinate love of self is the source of all sin and darkens the judgement ; for when will and sensibility are ill-disposed (that is, when they tend to pride and sensuality) everything that is in conformity with these inclinations appears to be good ' (I–IIæ, Q. lxxvii, art. 4).

[2] Ch. 75.

shalt love the Lord thy God with thy whole heart
and with thy whole soul and with all thy strength
and with all thy mind.'[1]   This commandment
requires the love of God for His own sake, and not
from self-interest or attachment to our own personal
satisfaction ; it demands, moreover, that we love
God with *all our strength* in the hour of trial, so
that we may finally arrive at the stage of loving Him
with our whole mind, when our love will be unaffected
by the ebb and flow of sensibility and we shall be of
those who ' adore in spirit and in truth.' Further-
more, this commandment is absolute and without
limits : the end for which all Christians are required
to strive is the perfection of charity, each in his own
condition and state of life, whether it be in the state
of marriage or in the priestly or the religious life.

St. Catherine of Siena emphasizes this in the 11th
and 47th chapters of her *Dialogue*, reminding us
that we can only perfectly fulfil the commandment
of love towards God and our neighbour if we have
the spirit of the counsels, that is to say, the spirit
of detachment from earthly goods, which, in the
words of St. Paul, we must use as though we used
them not.

The great motive of the second conversion is thus
described in the 60th chapter : ' Such souls should
leave their mercenary love and become sons, and
serve Me irrespective of their own personal advantage. I am the rewarder of every labour, and I
render to every man according to his condition and
according to his works. Wherefore, if these souls
do not abandon the exercise of holy prayer and their
other good works, but continue with perseverance to
increase their virtues, they will arrive at the state of
filial love, because I respond to them with the same
love with which they love Me ; so that if they love

[1] Luke x, 27.

Me as a servant loves his master, I pay them their wages according to their deserts, but I do not reveal myself to them, because secrets are revealed to a friend who has become one thing with his friend, and not to a servant. . . .

'But if My servants, through displeasure at their imperfection and through love of virtue, dig up with hatred the root of spiritual self-love, and mount to the throne of conscience, reasoning with themselves so as to quell the motions of servile fear in their heart, and to correct mercenary love by the light of holy faith, they will be so pleasing to Me that they will attain to the love of the friend. And I will manifest Myself to them, as My Truth said in these words : " He who loves me shall be one thing with me and I with him, and I will manifest myself to him and we will dwell together." ' These last words refer to the knowledge of Himself which God grants by a special inspiration. This is contemplation, which proceeds from faith enlightened by the gifts, from faith united with love ; it is a knowledge which savours mysteries and penetrates into their depths.

A second motive which should inspire the second conversion is the *price of the blood of the Saviour*, which St. Peter failed to realize before the Passion, in spite of the words : ' This is my blood which is shed for you,' which Christ pronounced at the Last Supper. It was only after the Resurrection that he began to comprehend this. We read in the *Dialogue*[1] on this subject : ' My creatures should see and know that I wish nothing but their good, through the Blood of My only-begotten Son, in which they are washed from their iniquities. By this Blood they are enabled to know My truth, how in order to give them life I created them in My image and likeness and re-created them to grace with the Blood of My

[1] Ch. 60.

Son, making them sons of adoption.' This is what St. Peter understood after his sin and after the Passion of Christ ; it was only then that he appreciated the value of the Precious Blood which had been shed for our salvation, the Blood of Redemption.

Here we have a glimpse of the greatness of Peter in his humiliation ; he is much greater here than he was on Thabor, for here he has some understanding of his own poverty and of the infinite goodness of the most High. When Jesus for the first time foretold that he must go to Jerusalem to be crucified, Peter took his Master aside and said to Him : ' Lord, be it far from thee, this shall not be unto thee ! ' In speaking thus he had, all unconsciously, spoken against the whole economy of Redemption, against the whole plan of Providence, against the very motive of the Incarnation. And that is why Jesus answered him : ' Get behind me, Satan ; thou savourest not the things that are of God but the things that are of men.' But now, after his sin and after his conversion, Peter in his humiliation has an understanding of the Cross, and he sees something of the price of the Precious Blood.

And so we can understand why St. Catherine constantly speaks in her *Dialogue* and in her *Letters* of the Blood which gives efficacy to Baptism and to the other sacraments. At every Mass, when the priest raises the Precious Blood high above the altar, our faith in its redemptive power and virtue ought to become greater and more intense.

A third motive which ought to inspire the second conversion is the love of souls which need to be saved, a love which is inseparable from the love of God, because it is at once the sign and the effect of that love. This love of souls ought in every Christian worthy of the name to become a zeal that inspires

all the virtues.   In St. Catherine it led her to offer
herself as a victim for the salvation of sinners.   In
the last chapter but one of the *Dialogue* we read:
' Thou didst ask Me to do mercy to the world. . . .
Thou didst pray for the mystical body of Holy
Church, that I would remove darkness and persecution from it, at thine own desire punishing in thy
person the iniquities of certain of its ministers. . . .
I have also told thee that I wish to do mercy to the
world, proving to thee that mercy is My special
attribute, for through the mercy and the inestimable
love which I had for man I sent into the world the
Word, My only-begotten Son. . . .

' I also promised thee, and now again I promise
thee, that through the long endurance of My servants
I will reform My Spouse.   Wherefore I invite thee
to endure, Myself lamenting with thee over the
iniquities of some of My ministers. . . . And I have
spoken to thee also of the virtue of them that live like
angels. . . . And now I urge thee and My other
servants to grief, for by your grief and humble and
continual prayer I will do mercy to the world.'

The fruit of this second conversion, as in the case
of Peter, is a beginning of contemplation by a pro-
gressive understanding of the great mystery of the
Cross and the Redemption, a living appreciation of
the infinite value of the Blood which Christ shed
for us.   This incipient contemplation is accompanied
by a union with God less dependent upon the
fluctuations of sensibility, a purer, a stronger, a more
continuous union.   Subsequently, if not joy, at all
events peace, takes up its dwelling in the soul even
in the midst of adversity.   The soul becomes filled,
no longer with a merely abstract, theoretical and
vague persuasion, but with a concrete and living
conviction, that in God's government all things are

ordained towards the manifestation of His goodness.[1]
At the end of the *Dialogue* God Himself declares
this truth:[2] ' Nothing has ever happened and
nothing happens save by the plan of My divine
Providence. In all things that I permit, in all things
that I give you, in tribulations and in consolations,
temporal or spiritual, I do nothing save for your
good, so that you may be sanctified in Me and that My
Truth be fulfilled in you.' It is the same truth which
St. Paul expresses in his epistle to the Romans :
' To them that love God all things work together
unto good.'

This is the conviction that was born in the soul of
Peter and the Apostles after their second conversion,
and also in the souls of the disciples of Emmaus when
the risen Christ gave them a fuller understanding of
the mystery of the Cross : ' O foolish,' He said to
them, ' and slow of heart to believe in all things which
the prophets have spoken. Ought not Christ to have
suffered these things and so to enter into his glory ?
And beginning at Moses and all the prophets he
expounded to them in all the scriptures the things
that were concerning him.'[3] They knew Him in the
breaking of bread.

What happened to these disciples on the way to
Emmaus should happen to us too, if we are faithful,

[1] There is nothing easier than to be convinced in theory that
Providence ordains all things without exception unto good. But it
is rare to find that truth realized in practice when some unforeseen
disaster enters like a cataclysm into our lives. There are few who
are able to see in such an event one of God's greatest graces, the
grace of their second or third conversion. The venerable Boudon,
a priest held in high repute by his own bishop and by several bishops
in France, one day received, in consequence of a calumny, a letter
from his bishop suspending him and forbidding him to say Mass
or to hear confessions. He straightway threw himself on his knees
before his crucifix, thanking our Lord for a grace of which he felt
himself to be unworthy. He had achieved that concrete and living
conviction, of which St. Catherine speaks here, that in the divine
government *everything*, absolutely everything, is ordained to the
manifestation of His goodness.

[2] Ch. 166. [3] Luke xxiv, 25–27.

on the way to eternity. If for them and for the Apostles there had to be a second conversion, still more is such a conversion necessary for us. And under the influence of this new grace of God we too shall say: ' Was not our heart burning within us whilst he spoke in the way and opened to us the Scriptures ? ' Theology, too, helps us to discover the profound meaning of the Gospel. But the more theology progresses, the more, in a sense, it has to conceal itself ; it has to disappear very much as St. John the Baptist disappears after announcing the coming of our Lord. It helps us to discover the deep significance of divine revelation contained in Scripture and Tradition, and when it has rendered this service it should stand aside. In order to restore our cathedrals, to set well-hewn stones into their proper place it is necessary to erect a scaffolding ; but when once the stones have been replaced the scaffolding is removed and the cathedral once more appears in all its beauty. In a similar way theology helps us to demonstrate the solidity of the foundations of the doctrinal edifice, the firmness of its construction, the proportion of its parts ; but when it has shown us this, it effaces itself to make place for that supernatural contemplation which proceeds from a faith enlightened by the gifts of the Holy Spirit, from a faith that penetrates and savours the truths of God, a faith that is united with love.[1]

And so it is with the question with which we are dealing, the truly vital question of our interior life in God.

[1] Thus St. Thomas at the end of his life was raised up to a supernatural contemplation of the mysteries of the faith, such that he could not dictate the end of the *Summa Theologica*, the last part of the treatise on Penance. He could no longer compose articles with a *status quæstionis*, beginning with three difficulties, followed by the body of the article and by the answers to the objections. The higher unity which he had now attained made him view all theological principles more simply and more radiantly, and he could no longer descend to the complexity of a purely didactic exposition.

CHAPTER III

The Third Conversion or Transformation of the Soul: Entrance Into the Unitive Way

WE have spoken of the second conversion, which is necessary for the soul if it is to leave the way of beginners and enter upon the way of proficients, or the illuminative way. As we have seen, many authors hold that this second conversion took place for the Apostles at the end of the Passion of Christ, and for Peter in particular after his triple denial.

St. Thomas remarks in his commentary on St. Matthew[1] that this repentance of St. Peter came about immediately, as soon as his Master had looked upon him, and that it was efficacious and definitive.

Nevertheless, Peter and the Apostles were slow to believe in the resurrection of Christ, in spite of the account which the holy women gave them of this miracle so often foretold by Jesus Himself. The story they told seemed to them to be madness.[2]

Moreover, slow to believe the resurrection of the Saviour, they were correspondingly anxious, says St. Augustine,[3] to see the complete restoration of the kingdom of Israel such as they imagined would come to pass. This may be seen from the question which they put to our Lord on the very day of the Ascension: ' Lord wilt thou at this time again restore the kingdom of Israel ? ' But there was still much

---

[1] Ch. xxvi, 74. [2] Luke xxiv, 11.
[3] *In Joan.*, tract. 25, n. 3 ; *Serm.* 265, 2-4.

suffering to be undergone before the restoration of the kingdom ; and that restoration would be far superior to anything that they suspected.

And so spiritual writers have often spoken of a third conversion or transformation of the Apostles, which took place on the day of Pentecost. Let us see first what this transformation was in them, and then what it ought to be, proportionately, in us.

The Apostles were prepared for their third transformation by the fact that from the time of the Ascension they were deprived of the perceptible presence of Jesus Himself. When our Lord deprived His Apostles forever of the sight of His sacred Humanity, they must have suffered a distress to which we do not perhaps sufficiently advert. When we consider that our Lord had become their very life—as St. Paul says : ' *Mihi vivere Christus est* '— and that they had become daily more and more intimate with Him, they must have had a feeling of the greatest loneliness, like a feeling of desolation, even of death. And their desolation must have been the more intense since our Lord Himself had foretold all the sufferings that were in store. We experience something of the same dismay when, after having lived on a higher plane during the time of retreat, under the guidance of a priestly soul full of the spirit of God, we are plunged once again into our everyday life which seems to deprive us suddenly of this fulness. The Apostles stood there with their eyes raised up to heaven. This was no longer merely the crushing of their sensibility, as it was during the time of the Passion ; it was a complete blank, which must have seemed to take from them all power of thinking. During the Passion our Lord was still there ; now He had been taken away from them, and they seemed to be completely deprived of Him.

It was in the night of the spirit that they were prepared for the outpouring of the graces of Pentecost.

The Descent of the Holy Ghost upon the Apostles.

' *All these were persevering in one mind in prayer, with the women and Mary the Mother of Jesus. . . .*'

The Acts of the Apostles give us an account of the event : ' When the days of Pentecost were accomplished they were all together in one place. And suddenly there came a sound from heaven, as of a mighty wind coming ; and it filled the whole house where they were sitting. And there appeared to them parted tongues, as it were of fire, and it sat upon every one of them. And they were all filled with the Holy Ghost ; and they began to speak with divers tongues according as the Holy Ghost gave them to speak.'[1]

The sound from heaven, like that of a mighty wind, was an external sign of the mysterious and powerful action of the Holy Spirit ; and at the same time the tongues of fire which rested upon each of the Apostles symbolized what was to be accomplished in their souls.

It happens not infrequently that a great grace is preceded by some striking perceptible sign which arouses us from our inertia ; it is like a divine awakening. Here the symbolism is as clear as it can be. As fire purifies, enlightens and gives warmth, so the Holy Ghost in this moment most deeply purified, enlightened and inflamed the souls of the Apostles. This was truly the profound purging of the spirit.[2] And St. Peter explained that this was

[1] Acts ii, 1–4.
[2] It is in the light of what is said here of the grace that purifies and transforms that we should read the articles of St. Thomas on the gifts of understanding and wisdom, and on the purification which they bring about within us ; likewise the *Dark Night* of St. John of the Cross.

the fulfilment of what the prophet Joel had foretold : ' It shall come to pass in the last days (saith the Lord) I will pour out my Spirit on all flesh ; and your sons and your daughters shall prophesy. . . . And it shall come to pass that whosoever shall call upon the name of the Lord shall be saved.'[1]

The Holy Ghost already dwelt in the souls of the Apostles, but by this visible mission[2] He came into them to increase the treasures of His grace, of the virtues and the gifts, giving them light and strength in order that they might be capable of witnessing to Christ even to the ends of the earth, and at the peril of their lives. The tongues of fire are a sign that the Holy Spirit enkindled in their souls that living flame of Love of which St. John of the Cross speaks.

Then were the words of Christ fulfilled : ' The Holy Ghost whom the Father will send in my name, he will teach you all things, and will bring to your mind whatsoever I shall have said to you.'[3] Then the Apostles began to speak ' in divers tongues the wonderful works of God,' so that the foreigners who were witnesses of this marvel, ' Parthians and Medes, Elamites and inhabitants of Mesopotamia, Judæa and Cappadocia, Pontus and Asia . . . Jews, Cretes and Arabians . . . were all amazed and wondered, saying . . . We have heard them speak in our own tongues.'[4] It was a sign that they were now to begin to preach the Gospel to the different nations, as our Lord had commanded them : ' Go ye, and teach all nations.'[5]

The effects of the descent of the Holy Ghost.

The Acts show us what were these effects : the Apostles were enlightened and fortified, and their

[1] Acts ii, 17, 21. [2] Cf. St. Thomas, I, Q. xliii, art. 6, ad 1.
[3] John xiv, 26. [4] Acts ii, 8–12. [5] Matt. xxviii, 19.

sanctifying influence transformed the first Christians ; there was a transport of intense fervour in the infant Church.

First of all, the Apostles received a much greater enlightenment from the Holy Spirit regarding the price of the Blood of the Saviour, regarding the mystery of Redemption, foretold in the Old Testament and fulfilled in the New. They received the fulness of the contemplation of this mystery which they were now to preach to humanity for the salvation of men. St. Thomas says that ' the preaching of the word of God must proceed from the fulness of contemplation.'[1] This was most fully verified at that time, as we may see from the first sermons of St. Peter related in the Acts and from that of St. Stephen before his martyrdom. These words of St. Peter and St. Stephen recall the saying of the Psalmist : ' Thy word is exceedingly refined and thy servant hath loved it.'[2]

The Apostles and the disciples, men without education, were still asking on the day of the Ascension : ' Lord, wilt thou at this time restore the kingdom of Israel ? ' Jesus had answered : ' It is not for you to know the times or moments which the Father hath put in his own power. But you shall receive the power of the Holy Ghost coming upon you, and you shall be witnesses unto me in Jerusalem and in all Judæa and Samaria, and even to the uttermost parts of the earth.'[3]

And now behold Peter. He who before the Passion had trembled at the word of a woman, who had been so slow to believe the resurrection of the Master, now stands before the Jews, saying to them with an

---

[1] II-IIæ, Q. clxxxviii, art. 6 : ' Ex plenitudine contemplationis derivatur doctrina et prædicatio.'

[2] Ps. cxviii, 140.

[3] Acts i, 6.

authority that can come only from God : ' Jesus of
Nazareth, a man approved of God by miracles and
wonders and signs which God did by him in the
midst of you . . . this same being delivered up by the
determinate counsel and foreknowledge[1] of God, you
by the hands of wicked men have crucified and slain.
Him God hath raised up [as David foretold]. . . .
This Jesus God hath raised again, whereof all we are
witnesses . . . he hath poured forth this which you
see and hear. . . . Therefore let all the house of Israel
know most certainly that God hath made both Lord
and Christ this same Jesus whom you have crucified.'[2]
Herein lies the whole mystery of the Redemption.
Peter now sees that Jesus was a willing victim, and
he contemplates the infinite value of His merits and
of the Blood which He shed.

The Acts add that those who heard this discourse
' had compunction in their heart and said to Peter :
What shall we do ? Peter answered : Do penance
and be baptized every one of you in the name of
Jesus Christ, for the remission of sins. And you
shall receive the gift of the Holy Ghost.' And so it
came to pass, and on that day about three thousand
persons were converted and received the sacrament
of baptism.[3]

Some days later, Peter said to the Jews in the
temple, after the cure of a man who had been lame
from birth : ' The author of life you killed, whom
God hath raised from the dead ; of which we are
witnesses. . . . Our Lord Jesus Christ of Nazareth,
whom you crucified . . . this is the stone which was
rejected by you the builders, which is become the

---

[1] It is to be noted in this and similar texts that the immutable
counsel or plan of God is mentioned before His foreknowledge of
which it is the basis. God foresaw from all eternity the mystery of
the Redemption, *because* from all eternity He had decreed to bring
it about.

[2] Acts ii, 22–36.   [3] ii, 41.

head of the corner. Neither is there salvation in any
other. For there is no other name under heaven
given to men, whereby we must be saved.'[1]   In this
enumeration of the graces of Pentecost we must
notice chiefly, not the gift of tongues or other powers
of this kind, but rather that special illumination which
enabled the Apostles to enter into the depths of the
mystery of the Incarnation, and more particularly of
the Passion of Christ. This is the mystery of which
Peter could not bear the prediction, when Jesus said
that He was to be crucified : ' Lord, be it far from
thee ; this shall not be unto thee.'   And Jesus
answered : ' Thou savourest not the things that are
of God, but the things that are of men.'[2]   Now Peter
has an understanding of the things of God, and he
contemplates the whole economy of the mystery
of the redemptive Incarnation. And it is not only
he who is thus enlightened. All the Apostles bear
witness in like manner, and the disciples also, and the
deacon, St. Stephen, who, before being stoned to
death, reminded the Jews of all that God had done
for the chosen people in the time of the Patriarchs,
in the time of Moses and, since then, until the coming
of the Saviour.[3]

But the Apostles were not only enlightened on the
day of Pentecost ; they were also strengthened and
confirmed. Jesus had promised them : ' You shall
receive the power of the Holy Ghost coming upon
you.'[4]   Fearful before Pentecost, they are now full
of courage, even to the point of martyrdom. Peter
and John, arrested and haled before the Sanhedrim,
declare that ' there is no salvation in any other '
than in Jesus Christ. Arrested again, and beaten
with rods, ' they went forth from the presence of the

---

[1] Acts iii, 15 ; iv, 11-12.   [2] Matt. xvi, 22-23.
[3] Acts vii, 1-53.   [4] Acts i, 8.

council rejoicing that they were accounted worthy to suffer reproach for the name of Jesus. And every day they ceased not, in the temple and from house house, to teach and preach Christ Jesus.'[1] They all bore testimony to Christ in their blood. Who had given them the strength to do this? The Holy Spirit, by enkindling the living fire of charity in their hearts.

Such was their third conversion; it was a complete transformation of their souls. Their first conversion had made them disciples of the Master, attracted by the sublime beauty of His teaching; the second, at the end of the Passion, had enabled them to divine the fecundity of the mystery of the Cross, enlightened as it was by the Resurrection which followed it; the third conversion fills them with the profound conviction of this mystery, a mystery which they will constantly live until their martyrdom.

The transformation which the Apostles had undergone is shown also in their sanctifying influence, in the transport of intense fervour which they communicated to the first Christians. As the Acts show,[2] the life of the infant Church was a life of marvellous sanctity; 'the multitude of the believers had but one heart and one soul'; they had all things in common, they sold their goods and brought the price of them to the Apostles that they might distribute to each according to his needs. They met together every day to pray, to hear the preaching of the Apostles, and to celebrate the Eucharist. They were often seen assembled together in prayer, and men wondered to see the charity that reigned among them. 'By this,' our Lord had said, 'shall all men know that you are my disciples.'

Bossuet has given an admirable description of the

[1] Acts v, 41.   [2] ii, 42–47; iv, 32–37; v, 1–11.

fervour of the first Christians, in his third sermon for the feast of Pentecost : ' They are strong in the face of peril, but they are tender in the love of their brethren ; the almighty Spirit who guides them well knows the secret of reconciling the most opposite tensions. . . . He gives them a heart of flesh . . . made tender by charity . . . and He makes them hard as iron or steel in the face of peril. . . . He strengthens and He softens, but in a manner all His own.   For these are the same hearts of the disciples, which seem as diamonds in their invincible firmness, and which yet become human hearts and hearts of flesh by brotherly love.   This is the effect of the heavenly fire that rests upon them this day.   It has softened the hearts of the faithful, it has, so to speak, melted them into one. . . .

' The Apostles of the Son of God had once disputed concerning the primacy ; but now that the Holy Spirit has made them of one heart and one soul they are no longer jealous or quarrelsome.   It seems to them that through Peter they all speak, that with him they all preside, and if his shadow heals the sick the whole Church has its part in this gift and praises our Lord for it.'   In the same way we ought to regard one another as members of the same mystical body, of which Christ is the head, and, far from allowing ourselves to give way to jealousy or envy, we ought to rejoice with a holy joy in the good qualities of our neighbour ; for we profit by them as the hand derives advantage from what the eye sees, or the ear hears.

Such were the fruits of the transformation of the Apostles and the disciples by the Holy Spirit.

But was the Holy Spirit sent to produce these marvellous fruits only in the infant Church ?   Evidently not.   He continues the same work throughout the course of ages.   His action in the Church is

apparent in the invincible strength that He gives her ;
a strength which may be seen in the three centuries
of persecution which she underwent, and in the
victory that she won over so many heresies.

Every Christian community, then, must conform
to the example of the infant Church. What must
we learn from her ?

To be of but one heart and one soul, and to banish
all divisions amongst us. To work for the extension
of the kingdom of God in the world, despite the
difficulties with which we are confronted. To
believe firmly and practically in the indefectibility
of the Church, which is always holy, and never
ceases to give birth to saints. Like the early Christians
we must bear with patience and love the sufferings
which God sends us. Let us with all our hearts
believe in the Holy Spirit who never ceases to give
life to the Church, and in the Communion of Saints.

If we saw the Church as she is in the most generous
souls who live most truly the life of the Church, she
would appear most beautiful in our sight, despite
the human imperfections which are mingled with the
activity of her children. We rightly lament certain
blots, but let us not forget that if there is sometimes
mud in the valley at the foot of the mountains, on
the summits there is always snow of dazzling white-
ness, air of great purity, and a wonderful view that
ever leads the eye to God.

The purification of the spirit necessary for
Christian perfection.

Create a clean heart in me, O Lord.[1]

We have seen that the transformation of the
Apostles on the day of Pentecost was like a third
conversion for them. There must be something

[1] Ps. l, 12.

similar in the life of every Christian, if he is to pass from the way of proficients to that of the perfect. Here, says St. John of the Cross, there must be a radical purgation of the spirit, just as there had to be a purgation of the senses in order to pass from the way of beginners to that of proficients, commonly called the illuminative way. And just as the first conversion, by which we turn away from the world to begin to walk in the way of God, presupposes acts of faith, hope, charity and contrition, so it is also with the other two conversions. But here the acts of the theological virtues are much more profound : God, who makes us perform these acts, drives the furrow in our souls in the same direction, but much more deeply.

Let us see now (1) why this conversion is necessary for proficients, (2) how God purifies the soul at this stage and (3) what are the fruits of this third conversion.

The necessity of the purification of the spirit.

Many imperfections remain even in those who have advanced in the way of God. If their sensibility has been to a great extent purged of the faults of spiritual sensuality, inertia, jealousy, impatience, yet there still remain in the spirit certain ' stains of the old man ' which are like rust on the soul, a rust which will only disappear under the action of an intense fire, similar to that which came down upon the Apostles on the day of Pentecost. This comparison is made by St. John of the Cross.[1]

This rust remains deep down in the spiritual faculties of the soul, in the intelligence and the will ; and it consists in an attachment to self which prevents the soul from being completely united to God. Hence

[1] *Dark Night*, Book II, ch. vi.

it is that we are often distracted in prayer, that we are subject to sluggishness, to a failure to understand the things of God, to the dissipation of the spirit, and to natural affections which are hardly, if at all, inspired by the motive of charity. Movements of roughness and impatience are not rare at this stage. Moreover, many souls, even among those that are advanced in the way of God, remain too much attached to their own point of view in the spiritual life ; they imagine that they have received special inspirations from God, whereas they are in reality the victims of their own imagination or of the enemy of all good. They thus become puffed up with presumption, spiritual pride and vanity ; they depart from the true path and lead other souls astray.

As St. John of the Cross says, this catalogue of faults is inexhaustible ; and he confines his attention almost exclusively to those defects which relate to the purely interior life. How much longer would the catalogue be if we considered also the faults which offend against fraternal charity, against justice in our relations with our superiors, our equals or our inferiors, and those which relate to the duties of our state and to the influence which we may exert upon others.

Together with spiritual pride there remains often in the soul intellectual pride, jealousy, or some hidden ambition. The seven capital sins are thus transposed into the life of the spirit, to its great detriment.

All this, says St. John of the Cross, shows the need of the ' strong lye,' that passive purgation of the spirit, that further conversion which marks the entrance into the perfect way. Even after passing through the night of the senses, St. John says, ' these proficients are still at a very low stage of progress, and follow their own nature closely in the intercourse and dealings which they have with God; because the gold of their spirit is not yet purified and refined; they still think of God as little children, and feel and experience God as little children, even as St. Paul says, because they have not reached perfection, which is the union of the soul with God.   In the state of union, however, they will work great things in the spirit, even as grown men, and their works and faculties will then be divine rather than human.'[1] Before this third conversion has taken place we may still say of these souls, in the words of Isaias, that their justices are as a soiled rag; a further, and final, purification is necessary.

How does God purify the soul in this third conversion?

It seems that at first He strips the soul instead of enriching it.   In order to cure the soul of all spiritual and intellectual pride, and to show it what dregs of poverty it still has within, He leaves the understanding in darkness, the will in aridity, sometimes even in bitterness and anguish.   The soul then, says St. John of the Cross, after Tauler, must 'remain in the dark, in pure faith, which is dark night for the natural faculties.'[2]   St. Thomas often points out that the object of faith is that which is *not seen (fides est de non visis)*; it is dark.   And the Angelic Doctor adds that it is impossible for anyone to believe and to see the same thing under the same aspect; because what is believed, as such, is not seen.[3]   The soul has now to enter into the depths of faith and to rise to its heights, like the Apostles when they were deprived of the sensible presence of Christ after His ascension. As He Himself had told them: 'It is expedient to you that I go.   For if I go not the Paraclete will not come to you; but if I go I will send him to you.'[4]

[1] *Dark Night*, Book II, ch. iii.   [2] *Ibid.*, ch. iv.
[3] II–IIæ, Q. i, art. 5.   [4] John xvi, 7.

St. Thomas gives an admirable explanation of these words in his commentary on St. John ; he says that the Apostles, attached as they were to the humanity of Christ by a natural love, were not yet sufficiently filled with a spiritual love of His divinity, and therefore were not yet capable of receiving the Holy Ghost spiritually, as they must if they were to withstand the tribulations which they would meet when Jesus had deprived them of His perceptible presence.

At first, then, God seems to strip the soul in this purification, as in the preceding ; He seems to leave it in darkness and aridity. The motto of the soul must now be : ' Fidelity and abandonment.' It is now that the words of Christ will be fulfilled : ' He that followeth me walketh not in darkness, but shall have the light of life.'[1] Especially illuminated now by the purging light of the gift of understanding, the soul begins, as St. Paul says, ' to search the deep things of God.'[2]

Now humility and the theological virtues are purged of all human alloy. The soul experiences more and more, without seeing it, the infinite purity and greatness of God, who transcends all the ideas that we can form of Him ; it experiences likewise all the supernatural riches of the holy soul of Christ, which here on earth contained the fulness of grace, ' all the treasures of wisdom and knowledge.'[3] Like the Apostles on the day of Pentecost it has a glimpse of the depths of the mystery of the Incarnation and the Redemption ; it perceives something of the infinite value of the merits of Christ who died for us on the Cross. The soul now has a sort of living knowledge, an experimental perception, of the supernatural world, a new outlook upon it. And by contrast the

[1] John viii, 12.
[2] 1 Cor. ii, 10 : ' Spiritus enim omnia scrutatur, etiam profunda Dei. . . . Nos autem accepimus. . . . Spiritum qui ex Deo est, ut sciamus quæ a Deo donata sunt nobis.'
[3] Col. ii, 3.

soul becomes more conscious of its own poverty.
The chief suffering of a St. Paul of the Cross, of a
Curé d'Ars, at this stage, was to feel themselves so
distant from the ideal of the priesthood, which
loomed now so great before them in the dark night
of faith ; while at the same time they understood
better the great needs of those many souls that had
recourse to them, imploring their prayers and their
help.

This third conversion or purification is, evidently,
the work of the Holy Spirit, who illuminates the
soul by the gift of understanding. As with a light-
ning-flash during the night He illumines the soul
that He wishes to purify. The soul had said to Him
so often : ' Enlighten my eyes that I may never sleep
in death ' ;[1] ' O my God, enlighten my darkness ' ;[2]
' Create a clean heart in me, O God, and renew a
right spirit within my bowels. Cast me not away
from thy face, and take not thy holy spirit from me.
Restore unto me the joy of thy salvation and strengthen
me with a perfect spirit. I will teach the unjust
thy ways . . . and my tongue shall extol thy justice.'[3]

The purified soul addresses to Christ those words
which He Himself once uttered, and begs that they
may be fulfilled in itself : ' I am come to cast fire
on the earth ; and what will I, but that it be kindled ? '[4]
This third purification comes about, as St. John of
the Cross says, by ' an inflowing of God into the soul,
which purges it from its ignorances and imperfections,
habitual, natural and spiritual, and which is called
by contemplatives infused contemplation or mystical
theology. Herein God secretly teaches the soul and
instructs it in perfection of love, without its doing
anything or understanding of what manner is this
infused contemplation.'[5]

---

[1] Ps. xii, 4.   [2] xvii, 29.   [3] l, 12.
[4] Luke xii, 49.   [5] *Dark Night*, Book II, ch. v.

This great purification or transformation appears under different forms, according as it is in pure contemplatives like a St. Bruno, or in souls dedicated to the apostolate or to works of mercy, like a St. Vincent de Paul ; but in substance it is the same. In every case there is the purification of humility and the three theological virtues from every human alloy, so that the formal motive of these virtues takes increasing ascendancy over all secondary motives. Humility grows according to the process described by St. Anselm, and repeated by St. Thomas : ' (1) To know that one is contemptible ; (2) to feel affliction at this knowledge ; (3) to confess that one is despicable ; (4) to wish one's neighbours to know this ; (5) patiently to endure their saying so ; (6) to submit to being treated as worthy of contempt ; (7) to like being so treated.' So we have the example of St. Dominic, who by preference went to those parts of Languedoc where he was ill-treated and ridiculed, experiencing a holy joy at feeling himself made like our Lord, who was humbled for our sake.

Then the formal motives of the three theological virtues appear in all their sublime grandeur : *the supreme Truth that reveals, Mercy ever ready to help, sovereign Goodness, ever lovable for its own sake.* These three motives shine forth like three stars of the first magnitude in the night of the spirit, to guide us surely to the end of our journey.

The fruits of this third conversion are the same as those of Pentecost, when the Apostles were enlightened and fortified, and being themselves transformed, transformed the first Christians by their preaching— as we learn from the Acts of the Apostles, where we are told of the first sermons of St. Peter and of St. Stephen's discourse before his martyrdom.

The fruits of this third conversion are a true and

deep humility, and a living faith that begins to relish and savour the mysteries of the supernatural order— as it were, a foretaste of eternal life. Moreover, it produces a firm and confident hope in the divine mercy, which is ever at hand to help us. To attain to this perfection of hope, one must, as St. Paul says, have hoped against hope.

But the most perfect fruit of this third conversion is a very great love of God, a very pure and very strong love, a love that hesitates before no contradiction or persecution, like the love of the Apostles who rejoiced to suffer for the sake of our Lord. This love is born of an ardent desire for perfection, it is ' hunger and thirst after the justice of God,' accompanied by the gift of fortitude, which enables it to triumph over every obstacle. It is the perfect fulfilment of the commandment : ' Thou shalt love the Lord thy God with thy whole heart, with thy whole soul and with all thy strength and with all thy mind.'

Henceforth the *depth of the soul* belongs completely to God. The soul has now reached the stage of living almost continually the life of the spirit in its higher part ; it is now an adorer in spirit and in truth. The darkness of the night of faith is thus a prelude to the life of eternity : *quædam inchoatio vitæ æternæ*. It is the fulfilment of the words of Christ : ' If any man thirst let him come to me and drink. . . . Out of his belly shall flow rivers of living water.'[1] This is the living water that springs up into eternal life, the water which Jesus promised to the Samaritan woman : ' If thou didst know the gift of God . . . thou perhaps wouldst have asked of him and he would have given thee living water. . . . The water that I will give him shall become in him a fountain of water, springing up into life everlasting.'[2]

[1] John vii, 37.   [2] iv, 10, 14.

PRAYER TO THE HOLY GHOST

Holy Spirit, come into my heart ; draw it to Thee by Thy power, O my God, and grant me charity with filial fear. Preserve me, O ineffable Love, from every evil thought ; warm me, inflame me with Thy dear love, and every pain will seem light to me. My Father, my sweet Lord, help me in all my actions. Jesus, love, Jesus, love (*St. Catherine of Siena*).

(Anyone who has consecrated himself to Mary according to the formula of the Blessed Grignion de Montfort, and then also to the Sacred Heart, will find great treasures in a repeated consecration to the Holy Spirit. The whole influence of Mary leads us to intimacy with Christ, and the humanity of Jesus leads us to the Holy Spirit, who introduces us into the mystery of the adorable Trinity.)

PRAYER OF CONSECRATION TO THE HOLY GHOST

O Holy Ghost, divine Spirit of light and love, I consecrate to Thee my intellect, my heart, my will and my whole being for time and for eternity.

May my intellect be ever docile to Thy heavenly inspirations and to the teaching of the Holy Catholic Church of which Thou art the infallible Guide. May my heart be ever inflamed with the love of God and my neighbour ; may my will be ever in conformity with the divine will, and may my whole life be a faithful imitation of the life and virtues of our Lord and Saviour Jesus Christ, to whom, with the Father and Thee, Holy Spirit, be honour and glory for ever. Amen.

(*Indulgence of 300 days once a day, applicable to the souls in Purgatory*—Pius X. This consecration may be renewed by repeating only the first paragraph of the form.)

CHAPTER IV

The Problem of the Three Stages of The Spiritual Life in Ascetical and Mystical Theology

THIS chapter, written especially for theologians, will prove less useful for the majority of readers, who will find the substance of it explained more simply and easily in the following chapter.

One of the great problems of the spiritual life is the question how we are to interpret the traditional distinction of the three ways, *purgative*, *illuminative*, and *unitive*, according to the terminology of Dionysius, or the way of *beginners*, of *proficients*, and of *the perfect*, according to an earlier terminology.

Of this traditional division two notably different interpretations have been given, according as the infused contemplation of the mysteries of faith and the union with God which results from it were considered as belonging to the normal way of sanctity, or as extraordinary favours, not only *de facto* but also *de jure*.

Statement of the Problem.

The difference between the two interpretations may be seen if we compare the division of ascetico-mystical theology used until the second half of the eighteenth century with that given by several authors who have written since that time. It is evident, for example, if we compare the treatise of Vallgornera, O.P., *Mystica theologia divi Thomæ* (1662), with the two works of Scaramelli, S.J., *Direttorio ascetico* (1751) and *Direttorio mistico*.

Vallgornera follows more or less closely the Carmelite, Philip of the Trinity. He likens the division given by him to that used by previous authors, and confirms it by appeal to certain characteristic texts of St. John of the Cross on the moment at which the passive nights of the senses and of the spirit generally make their appearance.[1] He divides his treatise for contemplative souls into three parts:

1. *Of the purgative way, proper to beginners*, in which he treats of the *active purification* of the external and internal senses, the passions, the intellect and the will by mortification, meditation and prayer, and finally of the *passive purification of the senses*, where infused contemplation begins and leads the soul on to the illuminative way, as St. John of the Cross explains at the beginning of the *Dark Night*.[2]

2. *Of the illuminative way, proper to proficients*, where, after a preliminary chapter on the divisions of contemplation, the writer treats of *the gifts of the Holy Ghost* and of *infused contemplation*, which proceeds especially from the gifts of understanding and wisdom, and which is declared to be a legitimate object of desire for all spiritual souls, as being morally necessary for the complete perfection of the Christian life. This second part of the work, after several articles dealing with extraordinary graces (visions, revelations, interior speech) concludes with a chapter of nine articles on *the passive purification of the spirit*, which marks the transition to the unitive way. This, likewise, is the teaching of St. John of the Cross.[3]

3. *Of the unitive way, proper to the perfect*, where the author deals with the intimate union of the

---

[1] Cf. Philip of the Trinity : *Summa theologiæ mysticæ* (ed. 1874, p. 17).
[2] Book I, ch. viii and ch. xiv.
[3] *Dark Night*, Book II, ch. ii and ch. xi.

contemplative soul with God and with its degrees, up to the transforming union.

Vallgornera considers this division to be the traditional one, and to be truly in harmony with the doctrine of the Fathers, with the principles of St. Thomas and the teaching of St. John of the Cross, and with that of the great mystics who have written on the three periods of the spiritual life, and on the manner in which the transition is generally made from one to another.

Quite different is the division given by Scaramelli and the authors who follow him.

In the first place Scaramelli treats of Ascetics and Mystics, not in the same work, but in two distinct works. The *Direttorio ascetico*, twice as long as the second work, comprises four treatises : (1) The means of perfection ; (2) the obstacles (purgative way) ; (3) the proximate dispositions to Christian perfection, consisting of the moral virtues in the perfect degree (the way of proficients) ; (4) the essential perfection of the Christian, consisting of the theological virtues and especially of charity (the love of conformity in the case of the perfect).

This treatise of Ascetics hardly mentions the gifts of the Holy Ghost. And yet according to the common teaching of spiritual writers the high degree of perfection in the moral and theological virtues which is here described is unattainable without these gifts.

The *Direttorio mistico* consists of five treatises : (1) An Introduction, on the gifts of the Holy Ghost and the *gratiæ gratis datæ ;* (2) on acquired and infused contemplation, for which, as Scaramelli admits, the gifts are sufficient ;[1] (3) on the degrees of obscure infused contemplation, from passive recollection to the transforming union. (Here, in Chapter XXXII, Scaramelli admits that several authors teach

[1] Ch. xiv.

that infused contemplation may be desired humbly by all spiritual souls ; but he comes to the conclusion that in practice it is better not to desire it unless one has received a special call to it : ' *Altiora te ne quæ-sieris* ') ;[1]   (4) on the degrees of distinct infused contemplation (visions and extraordinary interior words) ; (5) of the passive purifications of the senses and of the spirit.

It is surprising not to find until the end of this treatise on Mystics a description of the passive purgation of the senses, a purgation which, for St. John of the Cross and the authors above quoted, marks the entrance into the illuminative way.

The difference between this new way of dividing ascetico-mystical theology and the old way obviously arises from the fact that the old authors, unlike the modern ones, maintained that all truly spiritual souls can humbly desire and ask of God the grace of the infused contemplation of the mysteries of the faith : the Incarnation and Passion of Christ, Holy Mass and Eternal Life, mysteries which are so many manifestations of the infinite goodness of God. They considered this supernatural and confused contemplation to be morally necessary for that union with God in which the full perfection of the Christian life consists.

Hence it may be wondered whether the new division, as propounded for example by Scaramelli, does not diminish both the unity and the sublimity of the perfect spiritual life. When Ascetics are separated from Mystics in this way, do we sufficiently preserve the *unity* of the whole which is divided ? A good division, if it is not to be superficial and accidental, if it is to be based upon a necessary foundation, must repose upon the definition of the whole which is to be divided, upon the nature of that whole. And

[1] Similarly Tr. I, ch. 1, n. 10.

the whole in question is *the life of grace*, called by tradition ' the grace of the virtues and gifts ' ;[1] for the seven gifts of the Holy Ghost, since they are connected with charity, are part of the supernatural organism,[2] and, as St. Thomas teaches, are necessary for salvation, *a fortiori* for perfection.[3]

Similarly, the new conception surely diminishes the *sublimity* of evangelical perfection, since this is dealt with under the head of Ascetics, without mention of the gifts of the Holy Ghost, and without mention of the infused contemplation of the mysteries of faith and the union with God which results from that contemplation. While the new method of treatment emphasizes the necessity of ascetics, does it not at the same time degrade it, *weakening the motives for the practice of mortification and for the exercise of the virtues*, because it loses sight of the divine intimacy to which the whole of this work should eventually lead ? Does it throw sufficient light upon the meaning of the trials, those prolonged periods of aridity, which generally mark the transition from one stage of the spiritual life to the other ? Does not the new conception diminish also the importance and value of mysticism, which, if it is separated thus from

---

[1] Cf. St. Thomas, III, Q. lxii, art. 2 : ' Utrum gratia sacramentalis addat aliquid super gratiam virtutum et donorum ' ; where we are reminded that habitual or sanctifying grace perfects the essence of the soul, and that from grace there proceed into the faculties the infused virtues (moral and theological) and the seven gifts of the Holy Ghost, which are to the soul like the sails of a ship intended to receive inspirations from heaven.

[2] I-IIæ, Q. lxviii, art. 5 : ' Sicut virtutes morales connectuntur sibi invicem in prudentia, ita dona Spiritus Sancti connectuntur sibi invicem in caritate ; ita scilicet quod qui caritatem habet, omnia dona Spiritus Sancti habet, quorum nullum sine caritate haberi potest.'

[3] I-IIæ, Q. lxviii, art. 2, where these passages of Scripture are cited : ' God loveth none but him that dwelleth with wisdom ' (Wisd. vii, 28), and ' Whosoever are led by the Spirit of God, they are the sons of God ' (Rom. viii, 14).

asceticism, seems to become a luxury in the spiritual life of a few favoured ones, and a luxury which is not without its dangers? Finally, and above all, does not this conception debase the illuminative and unitive ways, by regarding them simply from the ascetical point of view? Is it possible for these two ways normally to exist without the exercise of the gifts of the Holy Ghost, proportionate to the exercise of charity and the other infused virtues? Are there *six ways* (three ascetical ways which are ordinary, and three mystical ways which are extraordinary), and not only three ways, three periods in the spiritual life, as the ancients maintained? Does it not seem that, if ascetics is divorced from the illuminative and unitive ways, it becomes simply an *abstract* study of the moral and theological virtues? Or, if the progress and *perfection* of these virtues is treated in concrete— as is done by Scaramelli—is it not manifest, according to the teaching of St. John of the Cross, that this perfection is *unattainable without the passive purifica-tions* and the operation of the gifts of the Holy Ghost? On this matter we shall do well to remember the words of St. Teresa : ' According to certain books we ought to be indifferent to the evil which is spoken of us, and even rejoice more thereat than if we were well spoken of ; we ought to make little of honour, and be detached from our neighbour . . . and many other things of the same sort. In my opinion these are *pure gifts of God, these are supernatural graces.*'[1]

In order better to preserve the unity and sublimity of the interior life, such as the Gospels and the epistles reveal it to us, we propose the division which follows. It accords with that of the great majority of authors who wrote before the second half of the eighteenth century, and, by including an *imperfect form* of the illuminative and unitive ways, mentioned by St. John

[1] *Life,* c. xxxi.

of the Cross,[1] it also safeguards that portion of truth which, in our opinion, the more recent conception contains.

Proposed Division of the Three Stages of The Spiritual Life.

Above the condition of hardened sinners, above the state of those sensual souls who live in dissipation, conversion or justification sets us in the state of grace ; grace which sin ought never to destroy in us, grace which, like a supernatural seed, ought continually to grow until it has reached its full development in the immediate vision of the divine essence and in a perfect love which will last for ever.

After conversion there ought to be a serious beginning of the *purgative life*, in which *beginners* love God by avoiding mortal sin and deliberate venial sin, through exterior and interior mortification and through prayer. But in actual fact this purgative life is found under two very different forms : in some, admittedly very few, this life is *intense,* generous ; it is *the narrow way of perfect self-denial* described by the saints. In many others the purgative life appears in *an attenuated form*, varying from good souls who are a little weak down to those tepid and retarded souls who from time to time fall into mortal sin. The same remark will have to be made for the other two ways, each of which likewise is found in an attenuated and in an intense form.

The *transition* to the illuminative life follows upon certain sensible consolations which generally reward the courageous effort of mortification. As the soul lingers in the enjoyment of these consolations, God withdraws them, and then the soul finds itself in that more or less prolonged aridity of the senses which is known as the *passive purgation of the senses.* This purgation persists unceasingly in generous

[1] *Dark Night*, Book I, c. xiv.

souls and leads them, by way of *initial infused contemplation*, to the full illuminative life. In other souls that are less generous, souls that shun the cross, the purgation is often interrupted ; and these souls will enjoy only an attenuated form of the illuminative life, and will receive the gift of infused contemplation only at long intervals.[1] Thus the passive night of the senses is seen to be a second conversion, more or less perfect.

The *illuminative life* brings with it the obscure *infused contemplation* of the mysteries of faith, a contemplation which had already been initiated in the passive night of the senses. It appears under *two normal forms :* the one definitely *contemplative,* as in the many saints of the Carmel ; the other *active,* as in a St. Vincent de Paul, a contemplation which, by the light of the gifts of wisdom and counsel, constantly sees in the poor and abandoned the suffering members of Christ. *Sometimes* this full illuminative life involves, not only the infused contemplation of mysteries, but also certain *extraordinary graces* (visions, revelations, interior speech), such as those described by St. Teresa in her own life.

The *transition* to the unitive life follows upon more abundant spiritual lights, or an easier and more fruitful apostolate, these being, as it were, the reward of the proficient's generosity. But in them the proficient is apt to take some complacency, through some remnant of spiritual pride which he still retains. Accordingly, if God wills to lead the proficient into the perfect unitive life, He causes him to pass through the *night of the spirit*, a painful purgation of the higher part of the soul. If this is endured supernaturally it continues almost without interruption until it leads the soul to the perfect unitive life. If, on the other

[1] See *Dark Night*, Book I, c. ix and c. xiv ; *Living Flame*, 2nd stanza, v. 5.

hand, the proficient fails in generosity, the unitive life will be correspondingly attenuated. This painful purgation is the third conversion in the life of the servants of God.

The perfect unitive life brings with it the infused contemplation of the mysteries of faith and a passive union which is almost continuous. Like the preceding, this life appears under two forms: the one exclusively *contemplative*, as in a St. Bruno or a St. John of the Cross; the other *apostolic*, as in a St. Dominic, a St. Francis, a St. Thomas, or a St. Bonaventure. *Sometimes* the perfect unitive life involves, not only infused contemplation and almost continuous union with God, but also *extraordinary graces*, such as the vision of the Blessed Trinity received by St. Teresa and described by her in the VIIth Mansion. In this perfect unitive life, whether accompanied by extraordinary favours or not, there are evidently many degrees, ranging from the lowest to the highest among the saints, to the Apostles, to St. Joseph and our Lady.

This division of the three stages of the spiritual life is set out in the following table, which should be read beginning from below; the three purgations or conversions figure in the table as transitions from one stage to another.

The scheme may be compared with the doctrine of Tradition, and above all with the doctrine of St. Thomas, concerning the grace of the virtues and the gifts, and with that of St. John of the Cross on the passive purgations, on infused contemplation and on the perfect union, the normal prelude to the life of heaven.

We have seen also how it may be compared with the three ages of our bodily life : infancy, adolescence, and manhood, especially as regards the crises which mark the transition from one to another.

UNITIVE LIFE of the perfect
- Plenary
  - *Extraordinary*, e.g. with vision of the Blessed Trinity.
  - *Ordinary* { *purely contemplative* form. *apostolic* form.
- *Attenuated :* Intermittent union.

Transition : Passive purgation of the spirit, more or less successfully endured.

ILLUMINATIVE LIFE of proficients
- Plenary
  - *Extraordinary*, with visions, revelations, etc.
  - *Ordinary* { *purely contemplative* form. *active* form.
- *Attenuated :* Transitory acts of infused contemplation.

Transition : Passive purgation of the senses, more or less successfully endured.

PURGATIVE LIFE of beginners
- *Generous :* fervent souls.
- *Attenuated :* tepid or retarded souls.

Transition : First conversion, or *justification*.

The transition from one stage to another in the Spiritual Life.

The transitions from one stage to another in the spiritual life, analogous to similar transitions in our bodily life, are marked by a crisis in the soul ; and none has described these crises so well as St. John of the Cross. He shows that they correspond to the nature of the human soul, and to the nature of the divine seed, which is sanctifying grace. In the *Dark Night*,[1] after having spoken of the spiritual imperfections of beginners, he writes : ' The one night or purgation will be sensual, wherein the soul is purged according to sense, which is subdued to the spirit. . . . *The night of sense is common, and comes to many ; these are the beginners.*' Then he adds :[2] ' When this house of sensuality was now at rest—that is, was mortified—

---

[1] Book I, ch. viii.   [2] *Ibid.* ch. xiv.

its passions being quenched and its desires put to rest and lulled to sleep by means of this blessed night of the purgation of sense, the soul went forth to set out upon the road and way of the spirit, which is that of *progressives* and *proficients*, and which by another name is called the way of *illumination* or of *infused contemplation*, wherewith God Himself feeds and refreshes the soul, without meditation, or the soul's actual help. Such, as we have said, is the night and purgation of sense in the soul.'

The words that we have italicized in this passage are very significant, and they reproduce the original Spanish exactly.

St. John of the Cross then proceeds[1] to treat of the imperfections which are proper to progressives or proficients : natural roughness, outward clinging of the spirit, presumption, a remnant of spiritual pride—and he thus shows the need of the *passive purgation of the spirit*, another painful crisis, a third conversion which is necessary before the soul can enter fully upon the *life of union* which belongs to the perfect, to those who, as St. Thomas says, wish above all things to cleave to God and to enjoy Him, and yearn ardently for eternal life, to be with Christ.'[2]

This doctrine of the *Dark Night* is found also in the *Spiritual Canticle*, especially in the division of the poem and in the argument which precedes the first strophe.[3]

It is sometimes objected that this sublime conception of St. John of the Cross far transcends the ordinary conception given by spiritual writers, who speak less mystically of the illuminative life of proficients and of the unitive life of the perfect. It

---

[1] *Dark Night*, Book II, ch. ii. [2] II–IIæ, Q. xxiv, art. 9.
[3] See also str. 4, str. 6, str. 22, v. 1.

would seem therefore that the *beginners* of whom St. John speaks in the *Dark Night* are not the beginners in the spiritual life, whom writers generally have in mind, but rather those who are already beginning the mystical states.

To this we may easily reply that the conception of St. John of the Cross corresponds admirably with the nature of the soul (sensitive and spiritual) and also with the nature of grace, and that therefore the beginners of whom he speaks are actually those who are usually so called. To prove this it is enough to note the faults which he finds in them : spiritual gluttony, a tendency to sensuality, to anger, to envy, to spiritual sloth, to that pride which causes them to ' seek another confessor to tell the wrongs that they have done, so that their own confessor shall think that they have done nothing wrong at all, but only good ... desiring that he may think them to be good.'[1] The souls thus described are certainly beginners, not at all advanced in asceticism. But it must be remembered that when St. John of the Cross speaks of the three ways, purgative, illuminative and unitive, he takes them, not in their attenuated sense, but in their normal and plenary sense. And in this he follows the tradition of the Fathers, of Clement of Alexandria, Cassian, St. Augustine, Dionysius, and the great teachers of the Middle Ages : St. Anselm, Hugh of St. Victor, St. Albert the Great, St. Bonaventure and St. Thomas.

This is particularly apparent in the *traditional distinction of the degrees of humility*,[2] which, by reason of the connection of the virtues among themselves, correspond to the degrees of charity. This traditional gradation in humility leads to a perfection which is assuredly not inferior to that of which St.

---

[1] *Dark Night*, Book I, ch. ii.   [2] See above, p. 63.

John of the Cross speaks. St. Catherine of Siena, the author of the *Imitation,* St. Francis of Sales and all the spiritual writers reproduce the same doctrine on the degrees of humility, corresponding to the degrees in the love of God. All books on ascetics likewise say that we must rejoice in tribulations and in being calumniated ; but, as St. Teresa remarks, this presupposes great purgations, the purgations of which St. John of the Cross speaks, and can result only from faithful correspondence with the grace of the Holy Spirit.

The same is apparent in the *classic distinction,* preserved for us by St. Thomas, between *political virtues* (necessary for social life), *purging virtues* (*purgatoriæ*), and the *virtues of the purified soul.* Describing the ' purging virtues,'[1] St. Thomas says : ' Prudence despises all the things of the world in favour of the contemplation of divine things ; it directs all thoughts to God. Temperance gives up all that the body demands, so far as nature can allow. Fortitude prevents us from fearing death and the unknown element in higher things. Justice, finally, makes us enter fully into the way of God.' The virtues of the purified soul are more perfect still. All this, together with what the Angelic Doctor says elsewhere of the immediate union of charity with God dwelling in the soul, is certainly not less sublime than what St. John of the Cross was to write later on.

Finally, the division of the three stages of the spiritual life corresponds perfectly to the three movements of contemplation described by St. Thomas after Dionysius : (1) The soul contemplates the goodness of God *in the mirror of material creatures,* and rises to Him by recalling the parables which Jesus preached to beginners ; (2) The soul contem-

---

[1] I-IIæ, Q. lxi, art. 5.

plates the divine goodness in the *mirror of intelligible truths*, or the *mysteries of salvation*, and rises to Him by a spiral movement, from the Nativity of Christ to His Ascension ; (3) The soul contemplates sovereign Goodness *in itself*, in the darkness of faith, circling round again and again, to return always to the same infinite truth, to understand it better and more fully to live by it.

It is certain that St. John of the Cross follows this traditional path which so many great teachers had trodden before him ; but he describes the progress of the soul as it is found in contemplatives, and in the most perfect among them, in order to arrive, ' as directly as possible at God.'[1]   He thus shows what are the higher laws of the life of grace and of the progress of charity.   But these same laws apply in an attenuated form to many other souls as well, souls which do not reach so high a state of perfection, but which nevertheless make generous progress without turning back.   In all things, similarly, we can distinguish two ' *tempos*.'   For example, the medical books describe diseases as they are in their acute stage, but they also point out that they may be found in a modified or attenuated form.

In the light of what has been said it will be easier for us now to describe the characteristics of the three ways, with special reference to the purgations or conversions which precede each of them—purgations which are necessary even though the soul may not have fallen again into mortal sin, but remained always in the state of grace.

From this point of view we shall now study what exactly constitutes the spiritual state of the beginner, the proficient, and the perfect ; and it will become apparent that this is not merely a conventional

[1] Cf. P. Louis de la Trinité, O.C.D., *Le Docteur mystique ;* Desclée de Brouwer, 1929, p. 55.

scheme, but a truly vital process founded on the
very nature of the spiritual life, that is, on the nature
of the soul and on the nature of grace, that divine
seed which is the germ of eternal life: *semen
gloriæ*.[1]

[1] An interesting point in this connection is that which Pope
Pius X had in mind when, in prescribing an earlier age for First
Communion, he said : ' There will be saints among the children.'
These words seem to have found their fulfilment in the very special
graces which have been granted to several children, taken very early
into heaven, who are to-day proving to be the source of so many
vocations to the priestly and the religious life : such as little Nelly,
Anne de Guigné, Guy de Fontgalland, Marie-Gabrielle, T. Gugliel-
mina and several others in France and Belgium—souls that remind
us of the Blessed Imelda, who died of love while making her thanks-
giving after her First Communion. Our Lord, who said : ' Suffer
the little children to come unto me,' is able evidently to endow these
souls with great sanctity at a very early age ; He sows the divine
seed in greater or less abundance in souls, according to His good
pleasure. (See Collection *Parvuli*, Lethielleux, Paris.)

CHAPTER V

Characteristics of the Three Stages of The Spiritual Life

WE have seen the different conceptions which various writers have proposed of the three stages or periods of the spiritual life ; and we have seen which of these is to be regarded as the traditional one. There is, we have said, an analogy between these three stages of the life of the soul and those of the life of the body : infancy, adolescence and manhood ; and we have paid particular attention to the transition between one period and another, marked by a crisis analogous to that which, in the natural or physical order, occurs in life about the age of fourteen or fifteen and again at twenty or twenty-one. We have seen also how these different periods of the interior life have their counterpart in the life of the Apostles.

We now intend, following the principles of St. Thomas and of St. John of the Cross, to describe briefly the characteristics of these three periods, that of beginners, proficients and perfect, in order to show that these are successive stages in a normal development, a development which corresponds both to the distinction between the *two parts of the soul* (sensitive and spiritual), and to the nature of ' *the grace of the virtues and the gifts.*' This grace progressively permeates the soul with the supernatural life, elevates its faculties, both higher and lower, until the *depth of the soul*[1] is purged of all

---

[1] This expression, a favourite with Tauler, has the same meaning as ' the summit of the soul ' ; the metaphor changes according as the things of sense are considered as *exterior* or as *inferior*.

egoism and self-love, and belongs truly, without any reservation, to God. We shall see that the whole development is logical ; it is logical with the logic of life, the logic which is imposed necessarily by life's end and purpose : *Justum deduxit Dominus per vias rectas :* ' The Lord guides the just by straight ways.'

i

Beginners.

The first conversion is the transition from the state of sin to the state of grace, whether by baptism or, in the case of those who have lost their baptismal innocence, by contrition and sacramental absolution. Theologians explain at length in the treatise on grace what precisely justification is in an adult, and how and why it requires, under the influence of grace, acts of faith, hope, charity and contrition, or detestation of sin committed.[1] This purgation by the infusion of habitual grace and the remission of sins is in a sense the *type or pattern of all the subsequent purgations of the soul,* all of which involve acts of faith, hope, charity and contrition. Often this first conversion comes about after a more or less painful *crisis* in which the soul progressively detaches itself from the spirit of the world, like the prodigal son, to come back to God. It is God always who makes *the first step* towards us, as the Church has taught against the Semi-pelagians ; it is He who inspires the good movement in us, that initial goodwill which is the beginning of salvation. For this purpose, by His grace and by the trials to which He subjects the soul, He as it were ' tills ' the ground of the soul before sowing the divine seed within it ; He drives a first furrow therein, a furrow upon which He will

---

[1] Cf. Council of Trent (Denzinger, 798) and St. Thomas, I-IIæ, Q. cxiii art. 1–8 inclusive.

later return, to dig more deeply still and to eradicate the weeds which remain ; much as the vine-tender does with the vine when it has already grown, to free it from all that may retard its development.

After this first conversion, if the soul does not fall again into mortal sin, or at all events if it rises from sin without delay and seeks to make progress,[1] it is then in the purgative way of beginners.

The mentality or spiritual state of the beginner may be best described in function of that which is primary in the order of goodness, namely his knowledge of God and of himself, and his love of God. Admittedly there are some beginners who are specially favoured, like many great saints who have had greater grace in their early beginnings than many who are proficients ; just as in the natural order there are infant prodigies. But after all, they *are* children, and it is possible to say in general in what the mentality of beginners consists. *They begin to know themselves,* to see their poverty and their neediness, and they have every day to examine their conscience to correct their faults. At the same time they begin to know God, in the mirror of the things of sense, in the things of nature or in the parables, for example, in those of the Prodigal Son, the Lost Sheep or the Good Shepherd. Theirs is a direct movement up to God, not unlike that of the swallow when it rises up to the heavens uttering a cry.[2] In this state there is a love

---

[1] St. Thomas (III, Q. lxxxix, art. 5, ad 3) explains that recovery is proportionate to the fervour of contrition. That is to say, if a person had two talents before committing a mortal sin, and if his contrition has been only barely sufficient and imperfect in relation to his former goodness, he will perhaps recover only one talent (*resurgit in minori caritate*). To recover the same degree of grace and charity which he had lost he will need a more fervent contrition, proportionate to the sin and to his former sanctity.

[2] The beginner sometimes considers the goodness of God also in the mysteries of salvation ; but he is not yet familiar with these and it is not an exercise which is proper to his condition.

of God proportionate to the soul's knowledge; beginners who are truly generous love God with a holy fear of sin, which causes them to avoid mortal sin and even deliberate venial sin, by dint of mortifying the senses and concupiscence in its various forms.

When they have been engaged for a certain time in this generous effort they are usually rewarded by some sensible consolations in prayer or in the study of divine things. In this way God wins over their sensibility, for it is by their sensibility that they chiefly live; He directs it away from dangerous things towards Himself. At this stage the generous beginner already loves God ' with all his heart,' but not yet with all his soul, with all his strength, or with all his mind. Spiritual writers often mention the *milk of consolation* which is given at this period. St. Paul himself says :[1] ' I could not speak to you as unto spiritual but as unto carnal, as unto little ones in Christ. I gave you milk to drink, not meat; for you were not able as yet.'

But what happens, usually, at this stage? Practically all beginners, when they receive these sensible consolations, take too much complacency in them; they regard them as though they were an end in themselves, and not merely a means to higher things. They then become an obstacle to their progress; they are an occasion of spiritual greed, of curiosity in the things of God, of an unconscious pride which leads the recipient to talk about his favours and, under a pretext of doing good to others, to pose as a master in the spiritual life. Then, as St. John of the Cross says,[2] the seven capital sins make their appearance, no longer in their gross form, but in the order of spiritual things, as so many obstacles to a true and solid piety.

Accordingly, by a logical and vital transition, a

[1] 1 Cor. iii, 2.   [2] *Dark Night*, Book I, ch. i–vii.

second conversion becomes necessary, described by St. John of the Cross under the name of *the passive purgation of the senses*. Of this he says that it is ' common and comes to many ; these are beginners,' and that its purpose is to lead them into ' the road and way of the spirit, which is that of progressives and proficients . . . the way of infused contemplation, wherewith God Himself feeds and refreshes the soul.'[1] This purgation is characterized by a *prolonged aridity of the senses*, in which the beginner is deprived of all those sensible consolations in which he had taken too great complacency. If in the midst of this aridity there is an intense desire for God, a desire that He should reign in us, together with a fear of offending Him, then this is a second sign that it is a divine purgation. Still more so, if to this intense desire for God there is added a difficulty in praying according to the discursive method, and an inclination towards the prayer of *simple regard, with love*. This is the third sign that the second conversion is in progress, and that the soul is being raised up to a higher form of life, that of the illuminative way.

If the soul endures this purgation satisfactorily its sensibility becomes more and more subject to the spirit ; the soul is cured of its spiritual greed and of the pride that had led it to pose as a master ; it learns better to recognize its own neediness. Not infrequently there arise other difficulties pertaining to this process of purgation, for example, in study, in our relations with persons to whom we are too greatly attached, and from whom God now swiftly and painfully detaches our affections. At this time, too, there arise often enough grave temptations against chastity and patience, temptations which God allows so that by reaction against them these virtues, which reside in the sensible part of our nature, may become

[1] *Dark Night*, Book I, ch. viii ; Book I, ch. xiv.

more firmly and truly rooted in us. Illness, too, may be sent to try us during this period.

In this crisis God again tills the ground of the soul, digging deeper in the furrow which He has already driven at the moment of our first conversion : He is uprooting the evil weeds, or the relics of sin, ' *reliquias peccati.*'

This crisis is not without its dangers, like the crisis of the fourteenth or fifteenth year in the development of our natural life. Some prove faithless to their vocation. *Some souls do not pass through this crisis in such a way as to enter upon the illuminative way of proficients,* and they remain in a state of tepidity ; they are not in the proper sense beginners, rather they are retarded or tepid souls. In their case, the words of the Scriptures are fulfilled : ' They have not known the time of their visitation ' ; they have failed to recognize the time of their second conversion. These souls, especially if they are in the religious or the priestly state, are not tending to perfection as they should, and unconsciously they are stopping others from doing so, placing serious obstacles in the way of those who really desire to make progress. Communal prayer, instead of becoming contemplative, becomes mechanical ; instead of prayer supporting the soul, the soul has to support and endure prayer. Such prayer may even, unhappily, become anti-contemplative !

In those, on the contrary, who pass through this crisis successfully it is, according to St. John of the Cross, the beginning of infused contemplation of the mysteries of faith, accompanied by an intense desire for perfection. Then the beginner, under the illumination especially of the gift of understanding,[1] becomes a proficient and enters upon the illuminative way ; he recognizes his own poverty, sees the

[1] *Dark Night*, Book I, ch. xiv.

emptiness of honours and dignities and the things of this world; he detaches himself from these entanglements. This he must do, as P. Lallemant says, 'in order to take the step' which will lead him into the illuminative way. He now begins what is like a new life; he is like the child that becomes a youth.

It is true that this *passive purgation of the senses*, even in the case of those who actually enter upon it, may be more or less manifest and more or less successfully endured. St. John of the Cross remarks this, speaking of those who are less generous at this stage: 'This night of aridities is not usually continuous in their senses. At times they have these aridities; at others they have them not. At times they cannot meditate; at times they can . . . for not all those who consciously walk in the way of the spirit are brought by God to contemplation. . . . And this is why He never weans the senses of such persons from the breasts of meditations and reflections, but only for short periods and at certain seasons.'[1] In other words, they have only an attenuated form of the illuminative life. St. John of the Cross explains this later by their lack of generosity: 'Here it behoves us to note why it is that there are so few that attain to this lofty state. It must be known that this is not because God is pleased that there should be few raised to this high spiritual state—on the contrary, it would please Him if all were so raised. . . . When He proves them in small things and finds them weak and sees that they at once flee from labour and desire not to submit to the least discomfort or mortification. . . . He goes no farther with their purification . . . they would fain go farther on the road, yet cannot suffer the smallest things nor submit themselves to them. . . .'[2]

[1] *Dark Night*, Book I, ch. ix.   [2] *Living Flame*, stanza II, 23.

Such is the transition, more or less generously made, which leads to a higher form of life. So far it is easy to see the logical and vital sequence of the phases through which the soul must pass. This is no mechanical juxtaposition of successive states, but an organic development of life.

ii

Proficients or progressives.

The mentality of proficients, like that of the preceding, must be described in function of their knowledge and love of God. With their self-knowledge there is developed in them a *quasi-experimental knowledge of God.* They know Him, no longer merely in the mirror of the things of sense or of parables, but in the *mirror of the mysteries of salvation,* with which they become more and more familiar and which the Rosary, the school of contemplation, sets daily before their eyes. The greatness of God is contemplated now, no longer merely in the mirror of the starry heavens, in the sea or the mountains, no longer merely in the parables of the Good Shepherd or the Prodigal Son, but in the incomparably more perfect mirror of the mysteries of the Incarnation and the Redemption.[1] To use the terminology of Dionysius, employed also by St. Thomas,[2] the soul rises in a spiral movement, from the mystery of the Incarnation or the Infancy of Jesus, to those of His Passion, His Resurrection, His Ascension and His Glory ; and in these mysteries it contemplates the radiance of

---

[1] The proficient also contemplates the goodness of God in the things of nature and in the parables of the Gospel ; but this is not the exercise proper to his condition, now that he has become familiar with the mysteries of salvation. But he has not yet attained, unless it be rarely and transitorily, to that circular movement whereby the perfect contemplate the divine goodness in itself.

[2] II–IIæ, Q. clxxx, art. 6.

the sovereign Goodness of God, thus admirably communicating itself to us. In this contemplation, which is more or less frequent, the proficients receive an abundance of light—in proportion to their fidelity and generosity—through the gift of understanding, which enables them to penetrate more and more deeply into these mysteries, and to appreciate their beauty, at once so simple and so sublime.

In the preceding period or stage God had won over their sensibility ; now He thoroughly subjugates their intelligence to Himself, raising it above the excessive preoccupations and complications of merely human knowledge. He simplifies their knowledge by spiritualizing it.

Accordingly, and as a normal consequence, these proficients being thus enlightened concerning the mysteries of the life of Christ, *love God*, not only by avoiding mortal sin and deliberate venial sin, but *by imitating the virtues of our Lord :* His humility, gentleness, patience ; and by observing not only those commandments that are laid upon all, but also the evangelical counsels of poverty, chastity and obedience, or at any rate by keeping the spirit of these counsels, and by avoiding imperfections.

As happened in the preceding period, this generosity is rewarded, but no longer by merely sensible consolations, but by a greater abundance of light in contemplation and in the work of the apostolate ; by intense desires for the glory of God and the salvation of souls, and by a *greater facility* in prayer. Not infrequently we find in the proficients the prayer of Quiet, in which the will is momentarily held captive by the love of God. This period is marked also by a great facility in doing works for God, such as teaching, directing, organizing, and the rest. This is to love God, not only with the whole heart, but with the whole soul, with the whole of one's activities ; but not yet with the whole strength, nor with the whole mind, because God has not yet achieved complete dominion in that higher region of the soul which we call the spirit.

And what happens generally at this stage? Something similar to what happened in the case of the beginners who had been rewarded with sensible consolations. The proficient begins to take complacency—by reason of an unconscious pride—in this great facility in prayer, working, teaching, or preaching. He tends to forget that these are God's gifts, and he rejoices in them with a proprietary air which ill beseems one who adores in spirit and in truth. It is true that he is working for God, he is working for souls; but he has not yet sufficiently forgotten himself. An unconscious self-seeking and self-importance cause him to dissipate himself and to lose the sense of the presence of God. He thinks that his labours are being very fruitful; but it is not quite certain. He is becoming too sure of himself, he gives himself too much importance and is perhaps inclined to exaggerate his own talents, to forget his own imperfection and to be too greatly aware of the imperfections of others. Purity of intention, true recollection, perfect straightforwardness, are often lacking; there is something of a lie in his life. ' The depth of the soul,' as Tauler puts it, ' does not belong entirely to God.' God is offered an intention which really is only half given to Him. St. John of the Cross mentions these defects of proficients as they are found in pure contemplatives, who, he says, ' believe in vain visions . . . and presume that God and the saints are speaking with them,'[1] being deceived by the ruses of the evil one. Not less notable are the defects, mentioned, for example, by St. Alphonsus, which are found in apostolic men

[1] *Dark Night*, Book II, ch. ii.

entrusted with the care of souls. These defects in proficients become manifest especially in the obstacles which they are called upon to meet, or in differences of opinion which, even at this advanced period of the spiritual life, may cause vocations to be lost. It then becomes evident that the presence of God is not sufficiently borne in mind, and that in the search for God it is the self which is really being sought. Hence the need of a third purgation ; hence the need of that ' strong lye ' of the purgation of the spirit, in order to cleanse the very depth of the spiritual faculties.

Without this *third conversion* there is no entrance into the life of union, which is the adult age, the manhood of the spiritual life.

This new crisis is described by St. John of the Cross[1] in all its depth and acuteness, as it occurs in the great contemplatives who, in point of fact, usually suffer not only for the sake of their own purification, but for the souls for whom they have offered themselves. The same trial occurs also in proficients of the apostolic type, generous souls who have reached a high perfection ; but it is generally less obvious in them since it is mingled with the sufferings incident to their apostolic labours.

In what does this crisis essentially consist ?—In the soul being *deprived*, not only of sensible consolations, but of *its supernatural lights* on the mysteries of salvation, of *its ardent desires*, of that *facility* in action, in preaching and in teaching, in which it had felt a secret pride and complacency, and by reason of which it had been inclined to set itself above others. This is a period of *extreme aridity* not only as regards the senses, but as regards the spirit, in prayer and the recitation of the office. Temptations frequently occur during this stage, not precisely against chastity or patience now, but against the virtues that reside in the higher part of the soul, against faith, hope

[1] *Dark Night*, Book II, ch. 3 *seq.*

and charity towards one's neighbour, and even against charity towards God, whom the soul is tempted to regard as cruel for trying souls in such a crucible of torment. Generally during this period great difficulties occur in connection with the apostolate : detraction, failures, checks. It will often happen that the apostle is made to suffer calumnies and ingratitude, even from those souls to whom he has done much good, so that he may thus be brought to love them more exclusively in God and for God's sake. Hence this crisis, or passive purgation of the spirit, is like a mystical death ; it is the death of the old man, according to the words of St. Paul : ' Our old man is crucified with Jesus Christ, that the body of sin may be destroyed.'[1] It is necessary to ' put off . . . the old man who is corrupted according to the desire of error, and be renewed in the spirit of your mind, putting on the new man who according to God is created in justice and holiness of truth.'[2]

All this is profoundly logical ; it is the logical development of the supernatural life. ' Sometimes,' says St. John of the Cross, ' in the stress of this purgation the soul feels itself wounded and hurt by strong love. It is a heat that is engendered in the spirit, when the soul, overcome with sufferings, is grievously wounded by the divine love.' The love of God is as a fire that progressively dries up the wood, penetrates it, sets it alight and transforms it into itself.[3] The trials of this period are permitted

---

[1] Rom. vi, 6.   [2] Eph. iv, 22.

[3] The progress in the knowledge and love of God which characterizes this purgation is precisely what differentiates it from certain sufferings which bear some resemblance to it, such as those of neurasthenia. These neurasthenic sufferings may have of themselves no purging character, but they too may be endured with resignation and for the love of God. Similarly the sufferings which may be the effect of our own lack of virtue, the effect of an undisciplined and exaggerated sensibility, have no purging quality of themselves, although they similarly may be accepted as a salutary humiliation in consequence of our faults, and in reparation for them.

by God in order to lead proficients to a more lofty faith, to a firmer hope, and to a purer love ; for it is absolutely necessary that *the depth of their soul* should belong completely to God. This is the meaning of the words of Scripture : ' As gold in the furnace he hath proved them, and as a victim of a holocaust he hath received them.'[1] ' The just cried and the Lord heard them ; and delivered them out of all their troubles. The Lord is nigh unto them that are of a contrite heart. . . . Many are the afflictions of the just ; but out of them all will the Lord deliver them.'[2]

This crisis, like the preceding, is not without its dangers ; it calls for great courage and vigilance, for a faith sometimes reaching to heroism, a hope against all hope, transforming itself into perfect abandonment. For the third time God tills the ground of the soul, but this time much more deeply, so deeply indeed that the soul seems overwhelmed by these afflictions of the spirit, afflictions similar to those often described by the prophets, in particular by Jeremias in the third chapter of the Lamentations.

He who passes through this crisis, loves God, not only with all his heart and all his soul, but according to the scale of the Scriptural phrase, *with all his strength ;* and he now prepares to love Him ' with all his mind,' to become an ' adorer in spirit and in truth,' that higher part of the soul which should control the whole of our activity being now in some sort established in God.

iii

The Perfect.

What is the spiritual state of the perfect after this purgation, which has been like a third conversion for them ? *They know God with a knowledge which is*

[1] Wisd. iii, 6.   [2] Ps. xxxiii, 18–20.

quasi-experimental and almost continuous ; not merely during times of prayer or the divine office, but in the midst of external occupations, they have a constant sense of the presence of God. Whereas at the beginning man had been selfish, thinking constantly of himself and, unconsciously, directing all things to himself, the perfect soul thinks constantly of God, of His glory, of the salvation of souls and, as though instinctively, causes all things to converge upon that end. The reason of this is that he no longer contemplates God merely in the mirror of the things of sense, no longer merely in parables or even in the mirror of the mysteries of the life of Christ, for this cannot continue throughout the whole day ; but he *contemplates the divine goodness in itself,* very much in the way in which we constantly see light diffused about us and illuminating all things from on high. In the terminology of Dionysius, employed also by St. Thomas, it is a movement of contemplation, no longer straight nor spiral, but *circular,* like the flight of the eagle which, after rising to a great height, circles round and round, and hovers to view the horizon.

This simple contemplation removes those imperfections that arise from natural eagerness, from unconscious self-seeking and from the lack of habitual recollection.

The perfect know themselves no longer merely in themselves, but in God, their source and their end ; they examine themselves, pondering what is written of their existence in the book of life, and they never cease to see the infinite distance that separates them from their Creator. Hence their humility. This quasi-experimental contemplation of God proceeds from the gift of wisdom, and, by reason of its simplicity, it can be *almost continuous ;* it can persist in the midst of intellectual work, conversation, external occupations, such continuity being impossible in the case of a knowledge of God which uses the mirror of parables or that of the mysteries of Christ.

Finally, whereas the egoist, thinking always of himself, wrongly loves himself in all things, the perfect, thinking nearly always of God, *loves Him constantly*, and loves Him, not merely by avoiding sin and by imitating the virtues of our Lord, but ' by adhering to Him, enjoying Him, desiring, as St. Paul said, to be dissolved and to be with Christ.'[1] It is the pure love of God and the love of souls in God ; it is apostolic zeal, zealous beyond measure ; but humble, patient and gentle.   This is to love God, no longer merely ' with the whole heart, with the whole soul, with the whole strength,' but continuing up the scale, ' *with the whole mind*.'   For he that is perfect is no longer merely rising gradually to this highest region in himself ; he is established there ; he is spiritualized and supernaturalized ; he has now become truly ' an adorer in spirit and in truth.' These souls preserve peace almost constantly amidst even the most distressful and unforeseen circumstances, and they communicate it to others who are troubled.   This is why St. Augustine says that the beatitude of the peacemakers corresponds to the gift of wisdom, which, together with charity, holds dominion over these souls.   The great model of such souls, after the holy soul of Christ, is the Blessed Virgin Mary.

All this, so it seems to us, shows the legitimacy of the traditional division of the three periods of the spiritual life, as understood by a St. Thomas, a

---

[1] II–IIæ, Q. xxiv, art. 9.   Hence I would reply to M. H. Bremond that this adherence to God, a *direct* act, which is at the source of the discursive and reflex acts of the perfect, contains the solution of the problem of the pure love of God and its reconciliation with a legitimate love of self ; for this is truly to love oneself in God, and to love Him more than oneself.

St. Catherine of Siena, a Tauler, and a St. John of the Cross. The transition from one stage to another is explained by the need of a purgation which in actual fact is more or less manifest. These are not schemes artificially constructed and placed mechanically side by side; it is the description of a vital development in which each stage has its own *raison d'être*. If there is sometimes a misunderstanding of the division, it is because sufficient account is not taken of the defects even of generous beginners or of proficients; it is because the necessity of a second and even a third conversion is forgotten; it is because it is sometimes overlooked that each of the purgations necessary may be more or less satisfactorily undergone, and may thus introduce more or less perfectly into the illuminative or the unitive way.[1]

Unless due attention is paid to the necessity of these purifications it is impossible to form a just idea of what the spiritual condition of proficients and perfect must be. It is of the necessity of a new conversion that St. Paul was speaking when he wrote to the Colossians:[2] 'Lie not one to another; stripping yourselves of the old man with his deeds, and putting on the new, who is renewed unto knowledge according to the image of him who created him. . . . But above all these things have charity, which is the bond of perfection.'

---

[1] The Carmelite, Philip of the Holy Trinity, in the prologue of his *Summa theologiæ mysticæ* (ed. 1874, p. 17), also regards the passive purgation of the senses as a transition between the purgative and the illuminative way, and the passive purgation of the spirit as a disposition to the way of union. In this, as in many other things, Th. Vallgornera, O.P., has followed him, and even copied literally from his work. Anthony of the Holy Spirit, O.C.D., has done likewise, summarizing him in his *Directorium mysticum*.

[2] iii, 9–14.

CHAPTER VI

The Peace of the Kingdom of God:
A Prelude to the Life of Heaven

THOSE who follow the way of generosity, self-denial, and self-sacrifice which the saints have taught, will come at length to know and taste the joys of God's complete dominion within us.

Truly spiritual delights have their source in the cross, in the spirit of sacrifice which causes disordered inclinations to die in us and gives the first place to the love of God and the love of souls in God, which installs in the throne of our souls that charity which is the source of peace, the tranquillity of order. These deep joys cannot enter into the soul until the senses and the spirit have been purged and refined by tribulations and sufferings which detach us from things created. As we read in the Acts of the Apostles: 'Through many tribulations we must enter into the kingdom of God.'[1]

The divine awakening.

After the dark and painful night of the spirit there is, St. John of the Cross tells us, a divine awakening: 'The soul uses a similitude of the breathing of one that awakens from his sleep,' and says, 'How gentle and loving is . . . thine awakening, O Word and Spouse, in the centre and depth of my soul . . . wherein alone, secretly and in silence, Thou dwellest as its Lord.' This divine awakening is an inspiration of the Word manifesting His dominion, His glory and His intimate sweetness.[2]

[1] xiv, 21.   [2] *Living Flame*, st. IV, 3, 4.

This inspiration shows the face of God radiant with graces and the works which He accomplishes. ' This is the great delight of this awakening : to know the creatures through God and not God through the creatures ; to know the effects through the cause and not the cause through the effects.'[1] Then is the prayer of the Psalmist fulfilled : ' Arise, Lord, why sleepest thou ? ' ' Arise, Lord,' that is to say, remarks St. John of the Cross, ' do thou awaken us, and enlighten us, my Lord, that we may know and love the blessings that Thou hast ever set before us.'[2]

The same grace is described in the 39th Psalm : ' With expectation I have waited for the Lord, and he was attentive to me. And he heard my prayers and brought me out of the pit of misery and the mire of dregs ; and he set my feet upon a rock and directed my steps, and he put a new canticle into my mouth.'

In this ' powerful and glorious awakening ' the soul receives, as it were, an aspiration of the Holy Spirit, who fills it to overflowing with His goodness and His glory, ' wherein He has inspired it with love for Himself, which transcends all description and all sense, in the deep things of God.'[3]

These graces are a preparation for that other awakening of the supreme moment of death, when the soul issuing forth from the body will see itself immediately as a spiritual substance, as the angels see themselves. And the last awakening of all will be in the moment of entrance into glory, when the soul, separated from the body, sees God face to face, and sees itself in God. Happy the saints who go straight to heaven. While those about them are lamenting their departure, they have reached the end of their journey in the clearness of the vision that gives them joy. As the Gospel says, they have entered into the joy of their Lord.

---

[1] *Living Flame*, st. IV, 5.   [2] *Ibid.*, 9.   [3] *Ibid.*, 17.

The Living Flame.

Already here on earth the divine awakening produces in the soul of the perfect a flame of love which is *a participation of that living flame which is the Holy Spirit Himself.* ' This flame the soul feels within it, not only as a fire that has consumed and transformed it in sweet love, but also as a fire which burns within it and sends out flame. . . . And this is the operation of the Holy Spirit in the soul that is transformed in love, that His interior actions cause it to send out flames. . . . And thus these acts of the soul are most precious, and even one of them is of greater merit and worth than all that the soul may have done in this life apart from this transformation, however much this may be ; . . . it is the same difference as that between the log of wood that is enkindled and the flame which it sends forth. . . . In this state, therefore, the soul can perform no acts, but it is the Holy Spirit that moves it to perform them. . . . Hence it seems to the soul that whensoever this flame breaks forth . . . it is granting it eternal life . . . it teaches the soul what is the savour of eternal life . . . it causes the soul to experience the life of God, even as David says : My heart and my flesh have rejoiced in the living God.'[1]

This flame wounds the soul as it is given, but the wound is tender, salutary and, instead of causing death, it increases life ; for the soul is holiest that is most wounded by love. Thus St. John of the Cross says that ' this wound is delectable,' and he adds that this ' came to pass when the seraph wounded the soul of St. Francis (of Assisi) with love.'[2]

When the heart is thus burning with love for its God, the soul is contemplating lamps of fire which

[1] *Living Flame*, st. I, 20–22 ; cf. Ps. lxxxiii, 3.   [2] *Ibid.*, II, 12.

enlighten all things from on high. These are the divine perfections : Wisdom, Goodness, Mercy, Justice, Providence, Omnipotence. They are, so to speak, the colours of the divine rainbow which, without destroying one another, are identified in the intimate life of God, in the Deity, as the seven colours of the rainbow are united in the one white light from which they proceed. ' All these are one lamp, which is the Word. . . . This lamp is all these lamps, since it gives light and burns in all these ways.'[1]

The powers of the soul are then as though melted in the splendour of the divine lamps ;[2] it is truly a prelude to eternal life.

' The soul is completely absorbed in these delicate flames, and wounded subtly in each of them, and in all of them more deeply and subtly wounded in love of life, so that it can see quite clearly that that love belongs to life eternal, which is the union of all blessings. So that the soul in that state knows well the truth of those words of the Spouse in the Songs, where He says that the lamps of love were lamps of fire and flame.'[3]

The flame which the wise virgins must tend in their lamps is a participation of this flame.[4]

The following lines from a recent commentary on the Canticle of Canticles are worth pondering : ' The divine love is a consuming fire. It penetrates the soul to its depth. It burns and consumes, but it does not destroy ; it transforms into itself. Material fire which burns wood to its innermost fibres and iron to its last molecules, is an image of that fire, but how feeble an image ! At times, under the influence of a specially powerful grace, the soul that is on fire with divine love sends forth flames. They ascend straight to God. He is their principle as He is their end ; and it is for His sake that the soul is consumed

---

[1] *Living Flame*, st., III, 3.   [2] *Ibid.*, 9.
[3] *Ibid.*, 5.   [4] Cf. Matt. xxv, 4-7.

with love.   The charity that elevates the soul to
God is only a created, finite, analogical participation
of uncreated charity ; but it is nevertheless a real,
positive and formal participation of the substantial
flame of Jehovah.'[1]

We can understand, therefore, why St. John of
the Cross often compares the soul that is penetrated
by God with the union of air and fire in a flame,
which is nothing else but air on fire.   Doubtless
there is always an infinite distance between the
Creator and the creature, but God by His action
enters so intimately into the purified soul that He
deifies it, giving it an increase of sanctifying grace.
And sanctifying grace is a real and formal participation of His inner life, His own nature, which is Deity.

Unitive love then becomes in the soul like a sea of
fire that ' reaches to the farthest heights and depths,
filling it wholly with love.'[2]   This love, hardly
perceptible at first, grows more and more until the
soul experiences an ever-increasing hunger for God
and a burning thirst, of which the Psalmist says:
' For thee my soul hath thirsted ; for thee my flesh,
O, how many ways ! '[3]   This is truly the beatitude
of those that hunger and thirst after justice ; this is
truly the prelude to the life of heaven, truly a beginning of eternal life, ' *quædam inchoatio vitæ æternæ*,'
as St. Thomas has said.   This is the supreme, but
normal, development of the life of grace on earth,
the seed of glory, *semen gloriæ.*

What are we to conclude from this doctrine, which
may appear too sublime for us poor mortals ?

It would certainly be too sublime for us if we had
not received in baptism that life of grace which, in us

[1] *Virgo Fidelis*, by Robert de Langeac (Lethielleux, 1931), p. 279.
[2] *Living Flame*, st. II, 9.
[3] Ps. lxii, 2 ; *Dark Night*, Book II, ch. xi.

too, must develop into eternal life ; if we had not often received Holy Communion, the precise effect of which is to increase that grace within us. Let us remind ourselves that each of our Communions ought to be substantially more fervent than the preceding, since each of them ought to increase the love of God in us, and thus dispose us to receive our Lord with a greater fervour of will on the following day.

As St. John of the Cross says,[1] spiritual souls that desire this union would attain it if they did not flee from those trials which God sends them for their purification.

Exactly the same doctrine is found in the *Dialogue* of St. Catherine of Siena, where we are given the explanation of those words of Christ : ' If any man thirst let him come to me and drink. . . . Out of his belly shall flow rivers of living water.'

' You were all invited, generally and in particular, by My Truth when He cried in the Temple, saying : " If any man thirst, let him come to me and drink. . . ." So that you are invited to the fountain of living water of Grace, and it is right for you, with perseverance to keep by Him who is become for you a bridge, not being turned back by any contrary winds that may arise, either of prosperity or adversity, and to persevere until you find Me, Who give the water of Life, by means of this sweet Word of love, my only-begotten Son. . . . '[2]

' But you must have thirst, because only those that thirst are invited. " If any man thirst," He says, " let him come to me and drink." He who has no thirst will not persevere, for either fatigue causes him to stop, or pleasure distracts him . . . he turns back at the smallest persecution, for he likes it not. . . .

[1] *Living Flame*, st. II, 23.   [2] Ch. 53.

The intellect must gaze into the ineffable love which I have shown thee by means of My only-begotten Son. . . . A man who is full of My love and the love of his neighbour finds himself the companion of many real virtues ; and then the soul is disposed to thirst : *it thirsts for virtue, and the honour of My name and the salvation of souls ;* every other thirst in him is spent and dead. The soul then walks securely . . . being stripped of self-love ; it is raised above itself and above transitory things. . . . It contemplates the deep love that I have manifested to you in Christ crucified. . . . The heart, emptied of the things that pass away, becomes filled with heavenly love which gives access to the waters of grace. Having arrived there, the soul passes through the door of Christ crucified and tastes the water of life, slaking his thirst in Me, who am the Ocean of Peace.'

What practical conclusion are we to draw from all this ? We ought to say and repeat this prayer to our Blessed Lord :

' Lord, teach me to know the obstacles that, consciously or unconsciously, I am placing in the way of Thy grace in me. Give me the strength to put them aside, and if I am negligent therein, vouchsafe Thyself to remove them, howsoever I may suffer thereby. What wouldst Thou have me to do for Thee this day, my God ? Show me what it is in me that displeaseth Thee. Teach me rightly to value the Precious Blood which Thou didst shed for me, of the sacramental or spiritual communion by which we are enabled to drink that Blood from the wound of Thy most loving Heart.

' Make me, O Lord, to grow in love of Thee. Grant that our inner conversation may never cease ; that I may never separate myself from Thee ; that I may receive all that Thou dost deign to give me ;

and that I may not stand in the way of the grace which through me should be poured out upon other souls to give them light and life.'

Pax in veritate.

And thus, in the words of St. Thomas, man lives no longer for himself, but for God.[1] He may say, with St. Paul : ' To me to live is Christ, and to die is gain.'[2] Life for me is not study, not work, or natural activity of any kind, but Christ.

Such is the way that leads to this quasi-experimental and almost continuous knowledge of the Blessed Trinity dwelling within us. And this is what makes St. Catherine say at the end of her *Dialogue :*[3]

' O eternal Trinity, O Godhead, O divine Nature that gavest to the Blood of Thy Son so great a price, Thou, O eternal Trinity, art a bottomless sea into which the more I plunge the more I find, and the more I find the more I seek Thee still. Of Thee it is never possible to say : Enough. The soul that is sated in Thy depths desires Thee yet unceasingly, for it hungers ever after Thee. . . . Thou art the fire that burns ever and is never quenched, the fire that consumes in itself all the self-love of souls, that melts all ice and gives all light. This light is an ocean into which the soul plunges ever more deeply and there finds peace.'

What better commentary could we find on those sublime words of St. Paul to the Philippians :[4] ' The peace of God, which surpasseth all understanding, keep your hearts and minds in Christ Jesus.' This is the fruit of the third conversion, in very truth a prelude to the life of heaven.

---

[1] II–IIæ, Q. xvii, art. 6, ad 3.   [2] Phil. i, 21.
[3] Ch. 167.   [4] iv, 7.

Note on the Call to
The Infused Contemplation of the
Mysteries of Faith

WE have pointed out above—and we have developed the theme at length elsewhere[1]—that the *seven gifts of the Holy Ghost are connected with charity*,[2] and that they consequently develop together with it. It is therefore impossible to have a high degree of charity without having at the same time and in a proportionate degree the gifts of understanding and wisdom, gifts which, together with faith, are the principle of the *infused contemplation* of revealed mysteries. In some of the saints, as in St. Augustine, this contemplation bears immediately upon the mysteries themselves ; in others, as in a St. Vincent de Paul, it bears upon the practical consequences of these mysteries; for example, upon the life of the members of the mystical body of Christ. But in either case it is infused contemplation. The superhuman *mode* of the gifts, a mode of activity which is derived from the special inspiration of the Holy Ghost and which transcends the human mode of the virtues,[3] is at first *latent*, as in the ascetic life ; but then it becomes *manifest* and *frequent* in the mystical life. In fact, the Holy Ghost usually inspires souls proportionately to their habitual docility or to their supernatural dispositions (i.e. according to the degree in which they possess

[1] *Perfection chrétienne et contemplation*, t. I, pp. 338–417 ; t. II, pp. 430–477.
[2] Cf. St. Thomas, I–IIæ, Q. lxviii, art. 5.
[3] I–IIæ, Q. lxviii, art. 1 ; see also *Perfection chrétienne . . .* t. I, pp. 355–385 ; t. II, pp. (52)–(64).

the virtues and the gifts).   This is definitely the
traditional teaching.

We have also shown elsewhere,[1] that according
to St. Thomas the gifts have not a human mode
specifically distinct from their superhuman mode ; for
if this were so, the former might always be perfected
without ever attaining to the latter, and would thus
not be essentially subordinate to it.

Now, if the gifts have no human mode specifically
distinct from their superhuman mode, it follows that
—as we have often said—there is for all truly spiritual
souls a *general remote* call or vocation to the infused
contemplation of the mysteries of faith—a contemplation which alone can give a profound and living
understanding of the redemptive Incarnation, of the
indwelling of God within us, of the sacrifice of
Calvary substantially perpetuated on the altar during
the Mass, and of the mystery of the Cross which
should be reproduced in any true and profound
Christian life.   However, this ' general and remote
call ' does not mean the same as an ' individual and
proximate call,' just as a ' sufficient call ' does not
mean the same as an ' efficacious call.'

We have recently been conceded, on this matter,
a point which we had not asked—and which, incidentally, we do not accept—namely, that ' the negative
element of perfection, that is to say, *detachment from
creatures, must be the same for all souls : complete,
absolute, universal' ;* ' there can be no degrees in
the absence of voluntary faults.   The very smallest,
like the very greatest, destroys perfection . . . a thread
is enough to hold a man captive.'

We do not think that detachment from creatures is
the same for all, whether for the greatest saints or for
those souls that have reached a minimal perfection.

---

[1] *Vie Spirituelle*, November, 1932 (Supplément, pp. (65)–(83) :
Les dons ont-ils un mode humain ?

And the principal reason is, that perfection excludes not only faults that are directly voluntary, but also those that are *indirectly voluntary ;* those which proceed from negligence and a relative tepidity, from a secret and semi-conscious egoism that does not allow the depth of the soul to belong completely to God. Likewise there is a certain co-relation between the intensive growth of charity and its extension, in consequence of which charity gradually excludes even those obstacles which we more or less unconsciously oppose to the work of grace in our souls.

If then, as we are granted, every soul is called by its progress in the love of God to exclude all voluntary faults, even the smallest, even those that are indirectly voluntary, it will succeed only by means of a high degree of charity. This charity will, evidently, be proportionate to the vocation of the individual soul ; it will not be the same for Bernadette of Lourdes as it was for St. Paul ; but it will have to be a high degree of charity. Without this the depth of the soul will not belong completely to God ; without this there will still be some egoism, which will manifest itself often enough by faults that are at least indirectly voluntary.

If a soul is to be perfect, it must possess a degree of charity higher than that which it possessed when it was still in the ranks of beginners or of proficients ; just as in the physical order the full age of manhood presupposes a physical strength superior to that of childhood or adolescence—though it may be that *accidentally* a youth is found to be more vigorous than a fully grown man.[1]

What conclusion follows regarding the *purgation of the depth of the soul,* which is necessary to exclude

[1] Non sunt judicanda ea quæ sunt per se, per ea quæ sunt per accidens.

all egoism and secret pride? A recent study on this question contains the following:

' I admit that the passive purgations (which are of the mystical order) are necessary in order to arrive at the purity required for mystical union; and it is in this sense that St. John of the Cross speaks. . . . But I deny that the passive purgations are necessary for the purity required in the union of love by conformity of wills.—The reason of this difference is a profound one. For the mystical union, which involves infused contemplation and love, active purgation is not sufficient, precisely because *the purity of the will* is not sufficient. It is necessary that there should be added to it a *sort of psychological purity* of the substance and the powers of the soul, which consists in rendering them adapted to the mode of being of the divine infusion.'

The important question, then, is: *Are the passive purgations, according to St. John of the Cross, not necessary for the profound purity of the will?* Are they not necessary in order to exclude that more or less conscious egoism, and those indirectly voluntary faults which are incompatible with the full perfection of charity, incompatible also with the full perfection of the infused virtues and gifts, which develop together with charity like so many functions of the same spiritual organism?

The answer to this extremely important question, for our part, is not for a moment in doubt.

It suffices to read in the *Dark Night*[1] the description of those faults of beginners which render the purgation of the senses necessary. Here are, not faults opposed to the *sort of psychological purity* of which our author speaks, but faults which are contrary to the *moral purity of the sensibility and of the will.* They are, in fact, as St. John of the Cross tells

[1] Book I, ch. ii–ix.

us, the seven capital sins translated into the order of
the spiritual life, such as spiritual greed, spiritual
sloth, spiritual pride.

The same remark may be made of the faults[1] of
proficients which render necessary the passive purgation of the spirit ; they are ' stains of the old man
which still remain in the spirit, like a rust which will
disappear only under the action of an intense fire.'
These proficients, says St. John of the Cross, are
really subject to natural affections ; they have
moments of roughness, of impatience ; there is still
in them a secret spiritual pride, and an egoism which
causes some of them to make use of spiritual goods in
a manner not sufficiently detached, and so they are
led into the path of illusions. In a word, the *depth
of the soul* is lacking, not only in psychological purity,
but in the moral purity that is required. Tauler has
spoken in the same sense, solicitous especially to
purify the depth of the soul of all self-love, of all
more or less conscious egoism. Hence it is our
opinion that the passive purgations are necessary
for this profound moral purity. But these purgations
are of the mystical order. They do not always appear
under so definitely contemplative a form as that
described by St. John of the Cross ; but in the lives
of the saints, even of the most active among them,
like a Vincent de Paul, the chapters which treat of
their interior sufferings prove that they all have a
common basis, which none has described better
than St. John of the Cross.

A final and very important concession has been
made to us in connection with the famous passage of
the *Living Flame*, st. II, 23 :

' It behoves us to note why it is that there are so
few that attain to this lofty state. It must be known

---

[1] *Dark Night*, Book II, ch. i and ch. ii.

that this is not because God is pleased that there should be few raised to this high spiritual state—on the contrary it would please Him if all were so raised—but rather because He finds few vessels in whom He can perform so high and lofty a work. For, when He proves them in small things and finds them weak and sees that they at once flee from labour, and desire not to submit to the least discomfort or mortification . . . He finds that they are not strong enough to bear the favour which He was granting them when He began to purge them, and goes no farther with their purification. . . .'

With regard to this it has recently been conceded : ' We admit that St. John of the Cross is treating here of the spiritual marriage, and that he states that the will of God is that all souls should attain to this state. But we deny that this implies a universal call to the mystical life. . . . The confusion arises, in our opinion, from a failure to distinguish two elements included by St. John of the Cross in the two degrees of union called *spiritual betrothal and marriage*. One of these two elements is essential and permanent ; the other accidental and transitory. *The essential element is the union of wills between God and the soul,* a union which results from the absence of voluntary faults and from the perfection of charity ; the *accidental element* consists in the actual union of the powers, a *mystical* union in the proper sense of the word, a union which cannot be continuous.'

In this supposition, it is possible that *the transforming union,* or spiritual marriage, should exist in a person *without that person ever having had a mystical union ;* the mystical union being merely an *accidental element,* like the interior words or the intellectual vision of the Blessed Trinity mentioned by St. Teresa.[1] To us, on the contrary, it appears certain

---

[1] *VIIth Mansion,* ch. i and ch. ii.

that, according to St. John of the Cross, the transforming union cannot exist without there having
been at least from time to time *a very lofty contemplation of the divine perfections*, an infused contemplation[1]
proceeding from the gifts, which have now reached a
degree proportionate to that of perfect charity. It
is, he says, ' even as the fire that penetrates the log
of wood . . . and having attacked and wounded it
with its flame, prepares it to such a degree that it can
enter it and transform it into itself.'[2]

Moreover, to our mind it is absolutely certain that
the *profound union of wills between God and the soul*,
which is recognized as being the essential element
of the transforming union, presupposes the *moral
purgation of the depth of the soul*, a purgation from
that more or less conscious self-love or egoism which
is the source at least of many indirectly voluntary
faults ; and this moral purification of the depth of the
soul, according to St. John of the Cross, *requires the
passive purgations* which eliminate the faults of
beginners and proficients.

We therefore maintain what we have said, in
common with numerous theologians, Dominican and
Carmelite, about the doctrine of St. Thomas and
St. John of the Cross concerning the gifts of the Holy
Ghost. To conclude, we recall especially these two
important texts :

' *The night of sense is common and comes to many ;
these are the beginners.*'[3] Being passive, this purification, or night, is of the mystical order : ' The way of
progressives or proficients . . . is called the way of

---

[1] According to St. John of the Cross (*Dark Night*, Book I,
ch. xiv) ' the way of illumination ' is a ' way of infused contemplation,
wherewith God Himself feeds and refreshes the soul.' *A fortiori*,
Man in the way of union.
[2] *Living Flame*, st. I, 16.
[3] *Dark Night*, Book I, ch. viii.

illumination or of infused contemplation, wherewith God Himself feeds and refreshes the soul.'[1]   Hence infused contemplation is in the normal way of sanctity, even before the unitive way is reached ; and therefore it is inconceivable that a soul should be in the state of spiritual marriage or the transforming union without ever having had that infused contemplation of the mysteries of faith which is the eminent exercise of the gifts of the Holy Ghost, developing in us side by side with charity.

We cannot admit that a mind of the calibre of St. John of the Cross can have meant only something *accidental* when he wrote the passage which we have just quoted, and which we quote once more in conclusion :

' The way of progressives or of proficients . . . is called the way *of illumination or of infused contemplation,* wherewith God Himself feeds and refreshes the soul.'

[1] *Dark Night,* Book I, ch. xiv.

THE END

If you have enjoyed this book, consider making your next selection from among the following . . .

Prices subject to change.

Prices subject to change.

At your Bookdealer or direct from the Publisher.
Toll Free 1-800-437-5876   *Fax 815-226-7770*
Tel. 815-226-7777   *www.tanbooks.com*

Prices subject to change.

Fr. Garrigou-Lagrange, O.P.
1877-1964

FATHER Reginald Marie Garrigou-Lagrange, O.P. (1877-1964) was probably the greatest Catholic theologian of the 20th century. (He is not to be confused with his uncle, Père Lagrange, the biblical scholar.) Fr. Garrigou-Lagrange initially attracted attention in the early 20th century, when he wrote against Modernism. Recognizing that Modernism—which denied the objective truth of divine revelation and affirmed an heretical conception of the evolution of dogma—struck at the very root of Catholic faith, Fr. Garrigou-Lagrange wrote classic works on apologetics, defending the Catholic Faith by way of philosophy, but especially by theology. Fr. Garrigou-Lagrange taught at the Angelicum in Rome from 1909 to 1960, and he served for many years as a consultor to the Holy Office and other Roman congregations. He is most famous, however, for his writings, having produced over 500 books and articles. In these he showed himself to be a thoroughgoing Thomist in the classic Dominican tradition.

Fr. Garrigou-Lagrange was best known for his spiritual theology, particularly for insisting that all are called to holiness and for zealously propounding the thesis that infused contemplation and the resulting mystical life are in the normal way of holiness or Christian perfection. His classic work in this field is *The Three Ages of the Interior Life*, in which the Catholic Faith stands out in all its splendor as a divine work of incomparable integrity, structure and beauty, ordered to raise man to the divine life of grace and bring to flower in him the "supernatural organism" of Sanctifying Grace and the Seven Gifts of the Holy Ghost— the wellsprings of all true mysticism. Among his other famous theological works are *The Love of God and the Cross of Jesus, The Mother of the Saviour and our Interior Life*, *Providence*, *Predestination*, *Life Everlasting* and *Christ the Saviour*. His most important philosophical work was *God, His Existence and Nature: A Thomistic Solution of Certain Agnostic Antinomies*.

The works of Fr. Garrigou-Lagrange are unlikely to be equalled for many decades to come.